ESSENTIAL FRENCH WINE

THE GUIDE TO FINDING YOUR NEXT BOTTLE

JÉRÔME CORNET

ISBN: 978-1-7773481-1-3

To my grandfather Gilbert

CONTENTS

FOREWORD

You want to pick up a wine bottle, and you know that France produces some of the best wines in the world, so you go check out the store. There, you face an impenetrable wall of incomprehensible labels that tell you nothing about the wine, so you end up picking an Italian Pinot Grigio or a California Cab'; or maybe pick up a bottle of Bordeaux (those are good, right?) and end up disappointed.

You are not alone.

Unlike the rest of the world, Europe has a long tradition of labelling wines by where they come from rather than by what's in the bottle. Yet, France has over 400 appellations (including over 100 for Bourgogne only) and more than 1000 designations, so how can you remember them all ?

This book will help you make sense of all this complexity. At a first level, it will give you a general idea of the styles of wines produced in each region and then dive into each one to give you a better understanding of the appellations and what to expect from them.

The first part of the book sets the level on how grapes influence the wine in the bottle, as does the geography of where it is grown and the winemaking techniques used to produce the wine. While you may know some of it already, it will help place in context the attributes of each region. The second part is the explanation of each French-producing region which will give you both an overview, then a deep understanding of the wines produced there. Last the third part is a series of charts to help you pick a wine, whether you are looking for a specific style or an alternative to other wines, and the index where every appellation will be linked back to its region and matching explanation.

This is a book that is meant for people who want to know more about French wine, so it's not a book for total beginners, although this may be the first book you buy about wine. I will assume that you have already tasted some wines and know the basic concepts, for example what acidity in wine feels like, or that you are not totally confused by what we mean by 'body' for a wine. That said, this is not an overly technical book and is meant to be accessible even if at the expense of pedantic correctness: for example, you will see aromas and flavours used interchangeably, same for grape and variety and many more.

Last, I am a firm believer that most wine styles have their place when paired with the appropriate food, and one of the joys of discovering wine is to find out what makes a wine good, whether you personally like it or not.

And remember to try something new ! This is just a rough map to get you started, and wine is one of these pleasures that gets better the more you know about it.

INTRODUCTION

This book is organized in 3 parts.

The first part lays out the foundations to understand French wine and what makes it special. If you already know a lot about how wine is made, you probably will feel the desire to skim through it, but read at least the first chapter on labelling, this will help you find your way.

The second part describes the French regions where wine is grown, the grapes that are used in the local appellations and how they compare.

The last part is meant to be used as a reference; whether you are trying to pick which region produces wines that match your taste, or information about a specific appellation or *grand cru*, you will find it in this chapter.

PART I

WHAT MAKES FRENCH WINE SPECIAL ?

DECODING FRENCH WINE LABELS
HOW TO FIGURE OUT WHAT MATTERS

W hat makes French wine very confusing is that for the most part, the labels will say nothing about what's in the bottle. So if you pick up any bottle, how do you know what to expect ?

Let's start with the only directly useful information that must be printed on the label: the alcohol percentage. It's there because of taxes but producers can round it up or down; usually wines over 15% alcohol are subject to heavier taxes, so if you see 14.5% it may actually be more than 15% in reality. As a guideline, 11.5 to 13% would be considered a medium level of alcohol, more than this would he high and 9-11% would be low.

Second, many importers, and sometimes producers actually tell you what's in the bottle and which style is the wine. That's really useful, but depending on where you get your wine from, those descriptive labels can be few and far between.

. . .

The key to decode French labels is therefore to understand the provenance of the wine; with this understanding, you can deduce the grapes used and the style of wine to expect.

So where do you start ?

———

The French wine provenance pyramid

Wine provenance pyramid

Before we talk about provenance, we have to talk about the wine provenance pyramid. At the top of it is wine made in a specific style coming from a particular place (usually a village or a small region); the European Union calls this PDO (Protected Designation of Origin), and while some wine labels will include this, it's likely that they will use the French translation *AOP* (*Appellation d'Origine Protégée*) or even more likely the traditional French labelling AOC (*Appellation d'Origine Contrôlée*). A lot of this book will be focused on AOC wines as each appellation (AOC) has to be made in a specific style from specific grapes, and is the top of the quality pyramid. In this book appellations will be written in **bold** and we will use the AOC terminology.

. . .

Next level down, is PGI (Protected Geographic Indication), which is labelled in French as IGP (*Indication Géographique Protégée*), although many producers are still using the traditional *Vin de Pays* (VdP) labelling, especially in the large **Vin de Pays d'Oc** designation. These wines must be made from grapes grown in larger region than appellations, and usually the set of grapes used is much wider and the blend formulas not regulated. It's usually the source of fairly inexpensive wines where you can get some expectation of quality, but is usually one notch below AOC. That said, some cult producers have eschewed AOC rules and bottle the wines they make as IGP so that they can use a different blend formula.

At the bottom of the provenance pyramid is also the bottom of the quality pyramid is the *Vin de France* or wine without geographic indication. If you see Vin de France on a label but is also accompanied with Appellation Contrôlée, or Vin de Pays or IGP, this indicates the higher echelons. But Vin de France on its own without the others means that the grapes can be grown anywhere in France and are usually low quality, so stay away from those.

Recognizing appellations

Looking at a label, how can you tell which is which ?

If it's an AOC wine, it will have the words *Appellation* and *Contrôlée* (or sometimes *Protégée*) on the label, although not always easily readable. Let's take Bordeaux for example: it may show up on a label as Appellation Bordeaux Contrôlée, Appellation d'Origine Contrôlée Bordeaux, AOC Bordeaux or Bordeaux AOC, but also possibly Appellation Bordeaux Protégée, AOP Bordeaux, Bordeaux AOP etc...

In this book, appellations will be bolded, so Bordeaux will refer to the town or the region, and **Bordeaux** the wine appellation.

If it's an IGP wine, it will have either the traditional *Vin de Pays* designation or the new *IGP / Indication Géographique Protégée* on the label. For example **Vin de Pays des Côtes Catalanes**, or **IGP Côtes Catalanes**. Confusingly, the largest IGP (along with a few others) include *Pays* in its name: Pays d'Oc; so for those, they will be labelled **Vin de Pays d'Oc** or **IGP Pays d'Oc**. Most of the wine we will discuss is AOC wine, some of it is IGP so in this book I will refer to it as the generic word appellation (whether AOC or IGP).

On many labels, this may not be the most prominent part of the label (the producer or wine name often is), so you may have to do some searching. It's usually mentioned on the front label, but sometimes on the back label.

This is the most important part of the label, and all throughout the book I will talk about appellations and what they taste like, so this is the key information to extract from a label. Some appellations, notably in Alsace, mandate putting the grape used on the label (**Alsace AOC Riesling**), and many IGP wines are varietally labeled (they name the grape). But for the most part the label will not tell you what is inside the bottle. This book will guide you so you can understand what goes in which appellation.

————

Grand Cru, Premier Cru

Cru is another indicator of quality that is regulated. Confusingly, there are 2 types of crus:

- *Grand Cru* and *Premier Cru* are given to the vineyard where grapes are grown, when proper production methods are followed.

- *Grand Cru Classé* or *Cru Classé* have been awarded to specific producers, most notably in Bordeaux (but also in Provence).

Grand Cru is the top-level echelon of the quality pyramid in a given appellation (they are often granted their own appellations) and is only granted to the very best best vineyards of a region (there are 51 in Alsace, 33 in Bourgogne). *Premier Cru* (sometimes labeled *1er Cru*), despite its name, is actually second best but is still of very high quality (there are 635 in Bourgogne only).

Grand Cru Classé usually includes a rank: *Premier* (or *1er*) *Cru Classé*, *Second* (or *2ème*) *Cru Classé*, all the way to fifth in Bordeaux, although most of those are simply labelled as *Grand Cru Classé* without mention of the rank. These so called "First Growths" are estates with a long standing wine production, but in this case *Cru classé* is not a more precise indicator of provenance. [1]

Cru Bourgeois and *Cru Artisan* are also denominations that indicate higher quality producers in Bordeaux (not vineyards) although most stand lower in the quality pyramid than the *Cru Classé*.

———

Sweet and sparkling wines

White still wines may be labelled with their sweetness indicator; while the rules are appellation-specific, the order goes this way:

sec, demi-sec, demi-doux, doux, moelleux, liquoreux

(dry, off-dry, semi-sweet, sweet, very sweet, luscious)

Confusingly, sparkling wines including Champagne use *Sec* to label semi-sweet wines, the dry variants are labelled *Brut*. So for sparkling wines, the order is:

---

brut nature, extra brut, brut, extra sec, sec, demi sec, doux

(no sugar, bone dry, dry, off-dry, semi-sweet, sweet, very sweet)

Vendanges Tardives (late harvest) is also a regulated indicator for sweet wines, as is *Sélection de Grains Nobles* specifically for Alsace. In both cases the grapes have been harvested when fully ripe and the sugar levels are really high.

As we will see in the winemaking section, there are 2 methods of production used in France for sparkling wines.

The *Méthode Traditionnelle* (traditional method) is used to produce most sparkling wines, but only Champagne wines can call it *Méthode Champenoise*.

The *Méthode Ancestrale* (ancestral method), is still used in some appellations under various other names (including *Pétillant Naturel* a.k.a. *PetNat*), but the easy way to recognize an ancestral method sparkling wine is that they are usually much lower in alcohol (6-8% vs 11-13%) and often cloudy rather than clear.

———

Organic, Biodynamic, Natural and other non-conventional methods

Most wine is still produced with "conventional" agricultural methods, including the use of pesticides in the vineyard, sulphites as a multipurpose agent during winemaking, and mechanical interventions like filtering and sometimes flash pasteurization to ensure a certain level of clean, crisp wines. While sulphites are a natural by-product of winemaking, they can be added to disinfect fermentation vats, to stop fermentation and as a preservative once the wine is bottled.

That said, there has been a growing movement over the last 50 years to reduce the amount of chemical and mechanical intervention both in the vineyards and the cellars. Unfortunately there is a whole slew of terms that describe some aspects of this management.

Certified organic wines will bear the label *Produit de l'Agriculture Biologique* (sometimes *A.B.*) or *Produit Bio* and means that the grapes followed the organic agriculture restrictions and follow a nationally-recognized certification process.

Biodynamic growing is a holistic approach to grape growing that is usually very manual and absent of chemicals, and most biodynamic producers (but not all) will be certified organic. While *Biodynamique* is not a state-regulated term, the winemakers that embrace these methods self-regulate their labels.

Agriculture raisonnée is another commonly found term on labels, and is also unregulated. It usually means that the grower only uses pesticides when a pest threatens the crops rather than preventatively. It's also used during the transition phase from conventional to organic agriculture.

Vin Méthode Nature is a new (starting with the 2019 vintage) regulated labelling term for natural wines, and means that the grapes have been produced organically, manually harvested, fermented without adding commercial yeasts, sulphites were not used before and during fermentation, and without using harsh filtration methods. The label is declined in 2 versions: *sans sulfites ajoutés* (with no added sulphites) and *avec moins de 30 mg/l de sulfites ajoutés* (less than 30mg/l of added sulphites, usually added as a preservative).

———

Other labelling terms

Réserve, Tradition, Château, Mas are often-used marketing terms that have no impact on the wine, so don't attach much importance to those.

Vieilles Vignes (old vines) is not regulated, but usually refers to wines over 20 years old, which tend to produce more concentrated, aromatic wines with lower yields.

One thing of note is the mention *Mis en bouteille à la propriété* or *Mis en bouteille au Château* (estate-bottled) which means that is was made by a grower-winemaker. If you see *Cave Coopérative* or *Les vignerons de...*, it means that it was it was made by a cooperative. While in some areas cooperatives are excellent, they tend to produce the average version of whatever appellation they are labelling, which is not necessarily for the best.

. . .

Now that you can decode a label, let's take a quick look at the grapes, how where they grow affects the wine and how the winemaker turns grapes into this delicious drink.

_____

1. The only appellation that mixes *Grand Cru* and *Grand Cru Classé* is St-Emilion in Bordeaux, but thankfully a wine must be a *Grand Cru* to be a *Grand Cru Classé*.

2

ENJOYING FRENCH WINE

DRINKING, EATING AND STORAGE

T hroughout this book, you will see descriptors of what wines
taste like. While words cannot convey the full complexity of
what's happening between in a glass of wine, there are attributes that
we look for in wines that helps differentiate them.

Acidity, Tannins, Body, Sweetness, Alcohol

I would argue that the most important attributes for a white wine are
acidity and body, and for red wines tannins and body.

But what are they exactly ?

Acidity is just that, the amount of acid in the wine. Acidity is what
makes your mouth water when you chew on a lemon. Too much of it,
and it makes you pucker, too little of it and the wine tastes flabby and
lifeless.

But how do you recognize acidity ? Part of the problem is that sweetness tends to mask acidity; a soda will taste refreshing because of its
acidity, but will not taste "acidic" despite the fact that most sodas are

objectively very acidic. So think of acidity as how fresh a wine tastes like. Does it zing and wakes up your senses, or is it more quietly sitting there, or even just flabby and dull ?

A fairly objective way to evaluate acidity is to make note of how much does a wine make your mouth water.

Acidity has also a different character depending on where it comes from; malic acid tastes like a green apple, while lactic acid tastes more like buttermilk or yogurt. Both will make your mouth water, but the former is more aggressive and "green", the later more well rounded.

Tannins come from the hard parts of the grape (skin, pips, stems) or barrels, and make your mouth dry and your tongue grippy. It's what makes black tea astringent, and gives the structure to many red wines.

Tannins have a magical ability to cut through fat, which makes red wines a popular accompaniment to fatty foods. Along with acidity, tannins are what gives wine its potential to age in a bottle. Low tannin wines are really smooth, medium tannins make your tongue grippy and you will feel high tannins up to your gums. But tannins are simply particles, so even when a wine has a lot of tannins, the tannins can be unripe and feel grippy and green, all the way to silken where they just contribute to the structure and mouthfeel of the wine without being disturbing.

Body is how heavy the wine feels in your mouth. Think of the differ-ence between skim milk and full fat milk: skim milk is light bodied, whereas full fat milk is full bodied. Many factors including the amount of alcohol, sugar, tannins and the nature of the acidity affect the perception of body in a wine.

. . .

Sweetness is really hard to gauge, so for this reason retailers will often list the perceived level if not the actual amount of sugar. Wines with under 4g/L of residual sugar are considered dry ("bone dry" on the low end), over 60g/L is lusciously sweet.

But to bring back the parallel with soda, the best sweet wines bring a lot of acidity to keep the wines refreshing despite the sweetness.

Interestingly, many red wines have a touch of residual sugar even though they are perceived as dry, but in that case the residual sugar is usually used to offset a high acidity or to give more body to the wine.

Alcohol is usually not a big factor in the taste of wines, although some wines will taste "hot", especially reds over 14%. Its biggest impact has more to do with how you feel the following day.

———

Pairing and Drinkability

The best wines are balanced. Powerful Bordeaux will have a high acidity, high levels of tannins, a full body and high intensity of aromas. Balance is easily noted when one of the attributes stands out -there is too much of it-.

Some wines are better when sipped alone (and usually have a touch of residual sugar), but many wines come on their own with food.

So how do you pair wine and food ?

Entire books have been written on the subject, but these tend to be the rules I use:

- The body of the wine should match the food: light fare with light bodied wines, hearty dishes with full bodied wines

- The wine should be more acidic than the food

- The wine should be sweeter than the food

- High tannins are great with fatty meat dishes

- Sparkling wines go well with salty foods

If you follow these simple guidelines you will get most of the way there.

———

Cellaring

Drink your wine. Seriously. Drink it.

Drink rosé within a year no matter what. For the most part, drink your wines within 1 to 3 years. Most wine is meant to be consumed young, and if it needs to be cellared many producers and distributors will cellar it until it's ready to drink.

Some great appellations can be kept for longer, and they will be mentioned throughout the book. But it's not because they can be kept that they should be kept; as they age, wine develops flavours that are more complex, but their intensity will fade so it's all a balancing act.

If you still need to store wine, the most important part of a cellar is how stable the temperature is. Of course, you can get a dedicated wine fridge, or maybe you have access to a cellar, but if not any room with a stable temperature will do. Avoid the kitchen (which tends to warm up when you cook) though.

3

GEOGRAPHY & LOCAL INFLUENCES
WHAT GOES INTO TERROIR

W hile a Gala or Granny Smith apple will pretty much taste the same regardless of which orchard it comes from, grapes have a unique way to taste differently based on where they are grown. There are multiple reasons for this: the weather patterns affects how grapes ripen and how much the taste and sugar is concentrated in the berries, but also the best wine comes from less fertile areas where the vine has to grow deep roots to extract nutrients and water from the soil.

France is uniquely placed in the world of wine because of the diversity of climate, soils and varieties that you can find throughout the country. In this chapter, we will discuss how the various aspects of the geography impact the wine that ends up in your glass.

Wine regions of France

Climate, weather and temperature

Climate is one of the most important aspects of winemaking: it affects not only which varieties can grow, but also how ripe or acidic they can be, to what style of wine you can make.

While there is no clear-cut definition of what a cool climate is vs. a warm climate (although if it snows in winter, it's probably a cool climate), you can think of France as being evenly divided: the wine producing regions in the northern half are cool climate regions, and in the southern half are considered to be warm climate regions.

Climate map of France

In cool climates, berries have a shorter time in summer to ripen, which keeps them more tart, green and less sweet. The Loire valley, Alsace, Savoie and northern Bourgogne all produce these delicious, light white wines where the acid combined with the lesser sweetness makes for a very refreshing zing on the palate.

Champagne is at the northern limit of France's wine growing regions, and unsurprisingly mostly produces sparkling wine. The defining characteristic of sparkling wine is the combination of bubbles with acidity, and the sweetness can be tweaked at the end of the wine-making process to accommodate consumer's taste (we'll talk about this in the next section).

In contrast, warm climates like you will find in the southern part of France (Languedoc-Roussillon, Provence, Corsica, Southern Rhône) help berries ripen, which concentrates the pigments in red wines and the sugar levels. Since winemaking is converting sugar into alcohol, the higher the sugar levels the higher the alcohol levels. This is why the south of France is packed with high alcohol, ripe reds.

Interestingly, some of the most famous regions are roughly in the middle latitudes: Bordeaux, Bourgogne and to some extent the Northern Rhône. For these, the weather for a given year has a huge influence on the resulting wine: a warm vintage will produce riper, fuller wines and tends to level the playing field between all the wine-makers, whereas a cold vintage will produce more acidic, sometimes thinner wines and lets the best winemakers stand out of the pack by only using wines from the best vineyards or better winemaking techniques to compensate for this.

This is why you will see vintage charts for these regions (hint: in good vintages, go for lesser known producers)

Local influences on climate

Large bodies of water often influence the local climate. Whether it's the Atlantic ocean in the Loire and Bordeaux, the Mediterranean sea all over the Southern Rhône, Languedoc-Roussillon, Provence and Corsica, they moderate the temperature to avoid extreme temperatures. In cooler climates, they limit the impact of cold temperatures including frosts, while in warmer climates they help bring some cool breezes to avoid drying the berries.

But it's not only seas and oceans: rivers play a major role in temperature regulation, like in the Loire and Northern Rhône and are sometimes keys to the production of certain wines: in Sauternes, the Ciron river, cooled by the Landes forest, creates morning fog when it joins the warm Garonne river, creating the unique conditions for the growth of *Botrytis Cinerea*, this fungus which concentrates the sugars of the most expensive wine in the world.

Rivers and seas

The terrain also influences widely the resulting wine: the best vineyards are often planted on slopes, so that the cool breezes of the night help preserve the acidity which contributes to the freshness of the wine, while during the day the exposure to the sun is often optimized. While many vineyards face south in the cooler climates, in warmer climates they often face another south-east or west, sometimes even north in hotter parts of France. Areas that have a big temperature range between day and night (called diurnal range) are usually prime areas for vineyards.

. . .

Mountains also have a big influence on the local climate. High altitude means cooler temperatures (and refreshing wines like in Savoie), but also they protect their eastern side from too much rain. This "rain-shadow" effect makes Alsace one of the driest wine producing regions in France despite its high latitude.

Last, dominant northerly winds, like the *Mistral* in the Rhône Valley and Provence, as well as the *Tramontane* in Languedoc and Roussillon bring a cooling and drying wine, which not only helps control acidity but also protects against various fungal diseases.

———

Soil composition

The composition of the soil can also have a big influence on the taste of the final wine, whether it's because some grapes just grow better on certain types of soils or because the same variety will taste differently in the glass depending on the soil it was grown on.

Some varieties just do better on a given type of soil given the same climate.

In Bordeaux, Cabernet Sauvignon and Merlot are both widely planted, but Cabernet tends to do better in gravelly or sandy soils which tend to be a bit warmer as they accumulate the heat of the sun during the day. Merlot tends to be planted on clay-rich or limestone soils which are a bit cooler.

In southern Bourgogne, Pinot Noir tends to be planted in soils with a higher content of limestone, whereas Chardonnay is usually planted on marly soils.

But in the cooler Champagne, Pinot tends to be planted on lime-stone-rich marly soils and Chardonnay tends to be planted in chalky soils.

However, the same grape planted on different soils can taste differently, so if the label mention which soil the grapes were grown in that is because it makes a difference.

Calcaire (limestone), while being an excellent regulator of humidity, brings out acidity and makes whites more mineral and reds fine and aromatics.

- Sauvignon Blanc in the Loire valley is very lean in Sancerre

- In Bourgogne, Chardonnay grown on limestone their acidity is often accompanied with a mineral character, especially in Chablis.

- In Champagne, chalk (a type of limestone) makes Chardonnay fine and elegant.

- In Bourgogne, Pinot Noir on limestone gives elegant, deeply aromatic wines if lighter in colour.

Argile (clay) or *Calcaire argileux* (marl) tends to bring out the wine's structure and power

- In Bourgogne, Pinot Noir on marl or clay give more structure and body at the expense of complexity.

- In Bourgogne, Chardonnay on marl gives powerful, concentrated whites,

- In Champagne Pinot Noir is usually planted in the limestone-rich marls to bring out its aromatics like in Bourgogne.

- In Pomerol and parts of Saint-Émilion, the clay soils can be very rich in iron which gives Merlot-based wines heady aromas of prune and walnut.

- When planted in clay or marls richer in limestone, Merlot brings out more red fruit notes to the wine.

- Rhône reds planted on clay soils tend to bring more tannins and age-worthiness

Gravel and *Galets* (large round rocks) are usually used for temperature management, where they absorb the heat of the sun during the day but reflect it at night, helping with ripening.

- They help Cabernet Sauvignon ripen on the right bank of Bordeaux and give its names to Graves

- They are used in the terraces of northern Rhône, especially in Crozes-Hermitage.

Silex, Granite and volcanic soils can bring out flinty, mineral notes to whites, and a distinct power

- Sauvignon Blanc gives aromas of flint when grown in the silex of Pouilly-Fumé

- Gamay in Beaujolais crus is mostly grown on granite soils which gives it a more concentrated flavour profile.

All of these factors, from geography to temperature to the composition of the soil and much more goes into what is called *terroir*.

4

VARIETIES

GRAPES IN THE BOTTLE

O ne of the most important components that affect the style of wine is the type of grape that goes into it. The technical term is variety, and wines made of a single variety are called varietal wines. Most of the wine grown in France uses so-called "International grapes" that are grown all over the world (even if many are native from France), so if you understand the variety or blend that is in a bottle, you should have a frame of reference.

This section highlights the principal grapes used in French wine so if you encounter a grape and you are not sure what it brings to the bottle, you can go back to this section and check. If you are looking for which variety to pick based on a taste profile, head over to Map of varieties (Chapter 17).

Red grapes

Merlot

It is the most planted grape in France, and while it makes easy drinking, fruit forward, red wines, it is used as a blending partner in many places, including in Bordeaux with Cabernet Sauvignon. It brings low acidity, high alcohol, moderately tannic and medium body with flavours of plum and cherry with cigar and baking spice aromas when aged in oak. Its home in France is Bordeaux and the south west of France.

Cabernet Sauvignon

The most planted grape worldwide, Cabernet Sauvignon bring tannins, acidity and body to the party. It is the core of first growth Bordeaux and many premium wines all over the world, from California to Australia. The aromas are reminiscent of black currant, more jammy in warm climates and with a hint of green pepper in cooler climates, but most notably it pairs wonderfully with oak, which brings out cedar and tobacco aromas.

Pinot Noir

If Cabernet Sauvignon and Merlot are reliable, in-your-face grapes, Pinot Noir is much more temperamental. It's fairly hard to grow (needs a Goldilocks-like not to warm but not too cool climate) and brings out the terroir it's grown in.

It usually makes high acidity wines, and in good years and in good hands it can deliver an incredibly complex red fruit flavours of cherry and strawberry, with sandalwood and smoke when aged in oak. But at its worst it's sour, thin and frustrating. The difficulty in growing Pinot explains the low yields and the high price that the wines tend to command, especially in its home of Bourgogne.

. . .

Cabernet Franc

The genetic parent of Cabernet Sauvignon and Merlot brings structure with its moderate levels of acidity, alcohol and tannins, and is often blended along with Cabernet Sauvignon. In the Loire valley red wines, Cabernet Franc is usually the star, where in Bordeaux and most of the south west, it remains a third player. Its tannins and quite high but usually very fine, and it brings herbal and red fruit flavours, and especially in the Loire aromas reminiscent of pencil shavings.

Syrah

Its home is in the Rhône Valley, particularly in the Northern Rhône (for example **Côte-Rôtie**) where it creates peppery wines with blue fruit flavours. It brings moderate levels of acidity and alcohols but high levels of tannins. It can bring leathery notes with age, and is also blended along with Grenache and Mourvèdre all over the South of France (in a blend nicknamed GSM or "Rhône Blend"). Australia makes powerful versions of wines, sometimes blended with Cabernet Sauvignon, where it is called *Shiraz*. While it is the same grape, producers all over the world tend to label Shiraz the more powerful, ripe style of the grape and Syrah for the more restrained French style.

Grenache

If Syrah brings blue fruit flavours, Grenache brings jammy/dried fruit to the party. Its best expression is in the Southern Rhône where it is blended in the GSM blend in appellations like **Châteauneuf-du-Pape**. It adds low acidity, high alcohol and moderate tannins which helps round the body of wines, especially when paired with Syrah. It is widely planted all over the South of France, and makes the unique *Vin Doux Naturels* (fortified wines) of **Maury** and **Banyuls**.

Lledoner Pelut is a mutation of Grenache which brings less alcohol and more acidity and is grown in Languedoc-Roussillon.

Gamay

Makes easy drinking wine with low tannins and high acidity. This is what **Beaujolais** is made out of, but it can also be found as a blending partner in the Loire valley rosés.

Mourvèdre

The third leg of the GSM blend, Mourvèdre brings animal notes, intense colour and high levels of acidity, alcohol and tannins. Native from Spain, it can be found all over the South of France; while a small amount goes a long way, it is the main grape in Provence's **Bandol** rouge.

Malbec

While Argentina made Malbec famous all over the world, its home is France where it is the base of **Cahors** wine where it is called *Côt*, and is often integrated as a blending partners all over the south west of France. It brings low acidity, soft tannins and a deep colour to the wine.

Carignan

Frequently added to the GSM blend, especially as you get closer to Spain, it used to be considered as a filler because of its high yields. But when grown with low yields, it produces structured wines with a deep colour, and its grippy tannins can be tempered by the use of carbonic maceration.

· · ·

Other grapes

Cinsault: Crafted into rosé or added to GSM blend especially in Rhône/Provence, Cinsault brings red fruit, low acidity and supple tannins.

Fer Servadou: similar to Cabernet Franc, it is found all over the French Southwest.

Grolleau: Usually blending partner for Loire rosé, sometimes used in Crémant as well.

Mondeuse Noire: Found in Savoie, it produces a deep colour and intense tannins, while bringing spicy, black cherry aromas.

Pinot Meunier: Mostly found in the **Champagne** blend where it expresses similar notes as Pinot Noir

Poulsard: Native from Jura, it makes lightly pigmented wines and is often vinified as a white.

Tannat: Intensely tannic, acidic, pigmented and full bodied, its home in France is **Madiran**, but can be found in southwest France blends.

———

White grapes

White grapes are traditionally split into aromatic vs not aromatic grapes. The so-called non aromatic grapes are probably what comes to mind when you think of a generic "white wine". Usually they bring some acidity, and citrus flavours.

Aromatic grapes bring in more exotic aromas of grape or lychee (Muscat or Gewurztraminer), herbaceous notes (Sauvignon blanc) or floral notes (Viognier). It's worth noting that the winemaker can dial the flavours of the aromatic grapes.

Chardonnay

Chardonnay is grown all over the world and is adaptable to a wide variety of climates. In France, it is grown everywhere, from Champagne to the Languedoc including of course Bourgogne. When fully ripe, it produces wines of high alcohol and high extract levels, but at the expense of acidity; it when grown on limestone and especially in cooler climates, acidity can remain with lower alcohol levels. The primary aromas of citrus and apple can be augmented with buttery, nutty flavours, especially when using oak and malo-lactic fermentation. Like Pinot Noir, this is a grape that expresses the terroir it comes from.

Sauvignon Blanc

The other parent of Cabernet Sauvignon brings a high acidity and herbaceous notes to the wine. While New Zealand's Sauvignon blanc can pack a punch with more grapefruit and kiwis aromas, French Sauvignon Blanc is usually more understated. It can be found all over Western France, in the Loire Valley where it brings more mineral and green pepper notes, and in Bordeaux (usually blended with Sémillon) where it's more muted and brings more orchard fruit flavours.

. . .

Chenin Blanc

While also fairly flexible in terms of climate, Chenin brings very high acidity, and moderate aromas of peach and apricot. Its thick skin makes it very accommodating to botrytis cinerea, which turns Chenin into sweet wines with levels of acidity, sugar and alcohol can make them cellar-worthy.

Pinot Gris

While mostly known in France for its Alsace rendition, the grape is also known as *Pinot Grigio* when crafted into a lighter, Italian style. In Alsace, it brings high levels of sugar, extraction and low acidity, with orchard fruit and nutty aromas.

Riesling

If Germany is famous for its Riesling, Alsace's best wines are made from this native grape. It prefers cool climates, but brings high acidity and sugar levels (and therefore alcohol). While this aromatic grape brings orchard fruit and floral notes, as it ages it brings a distinctive aroma of pine nut.

Muscat

Muscat is an entire family of grapes, but for the most part wine in France is made with Muscat Blanc à Petits Grains. It brings high levels of acidity with notes of raisin, honey, peach and apricot. It is used for *vin doux naturel* production in the South of France, as well as in Alsace where it is one of the noble grapes.

. . .

Other grapes

Vermentino: This Italian grape, known as *Rolle* in Provence and *Vermentinu* in Corse produces full bodied, wines with low acidity and rich notes of pear and almond.

Pinot blanc: A fairly neutral grape, bringing moderate levels of acidity and body.

Gewurztraminer: high sugar levels making it very suitable for late harvest, this very aromatic grape brings flora aromas of ginger, cardamom and lychee.

Viognier: this very aromatic grape makes wines high in alcohol and low to moderate in acidity. it can be found in the south, especially in the northern Rhône valley.

Roussanne: grown from Savoie to the south of France, it brings moderate levels of acidity with elegant and floral notes of honey and apricot.

Marsanne: often blended with Roussanne, it brings low to moderate acidity but high alcohol and high extract, with notes of melon.

Jacquère: the base of most white from Savoie, it produces high acidity, lightly perfumed wines.

. . .

Sémillon: Native from Sauternes, it's well suited for botrytis. The high alcohol, high extract and low acidity give body to the wine it makes.

Muscadet: Melon Blanc / Melon de Bourgogne, grown in the Loire Valley brings high acidity and a light body to the wine.

Folle Blanche: (Gros Plant) grown in the Lower Loire but used extensively for brandy production.

Picpoul (Piquepoul): The Muscadet of Languedoc, light and refreshing.

Clairette: low in acid but high in alcohol, it is used for sparkling wine production in the south.

Aligoté: gives high acidity, medium bodied wines with jasmine and vanilla aromas, can be found in Bourgogne.

Savagnin Blanc: used for *vin jaune* production, this ancient grape brings high levels of acidity and alcohol.

5

WINEMAKING
TURNING GRAPES INTO WINE

W e discussed grapes and terroir, let's now take a look at how wine is made, and what choices a winemaker has when producing wine.

Styles of wines

At a very basic level, wine is made by extracting the juice from grape berries, and converting the sugar it contains into alcohol.

There are a few choices in the process that a winemaker can make, and we will look into those.

Most berries, whether red or green on the outside, are clear inside so they can be used for white wine production. To make red wines, the juice is left in contact with the skins of the berries for a while, which impart their colour onto the resulting wine. Rosé wine is made (for the most part) by shortening the contact time to impart just a little colour.

. . .

Vin Tranquille (still wine) is probably what you think of when you hear the word wine. It means that it has no bubbles, and ranges from around 10 to under 15% abv (alcohol by volume). Wine can also be made sparkling (and labelled *Crémant, Mousseux* or *Pétillant*), or fortified (labelled *Vin Doux Naturel*) in which case the resulting wine will usually be from 16 to 20% abv.

Fermentation choices

Most winemakers use yeasts to convert grape juice into alcohol. The basic formula is:

---

sugar + yeasts + oxygen

=> carbon dioxide + alcohol

---

and when the sugar runs low or the alcohol level runs high, the yeasts die and fall at the bottom of the vat.

Looking at each element of this formula can tell us about the various choices a winemaker has.

1. Sugar

Sugar levels increases as the grape ripen, so does the potential alcohol levels, which is why wines from warm climates, which tend to be made with riper grapes, tend to have higher alcohol levels.

But the fermentation can stop before all the sugar has been converted, resulting in wines with various levels of sweetness, from off-dry if there is a bit too luscious for the sweetest wines.

There are 3 ways this happens; if there is a lot of sugar in the berries (think of late harvest wines), and the alcohol levels rise enough before all the sugar has been converted. Alternatively the winemaker can interrupt the fermentation by using sulphites when the right level of alcohol and sweetness has been reached, or by adding grape alcohol to artificially raise the alcohol level which will kill the yeasts. This is how fortified wine is made (fortification is the addition of alcohol).

2. Yeasts

The winemaker has a choice between using the natural (indigenous) yeasts that are present on the skins of the grapes, or using commercially available yeasts that are known to bring out specific aromas in the wine. *Vin Nature*, as well as many traditional wine growing regions use indigenous yeasts, while the bulk of wine is made using commercial yeasts.

But once they die, the yeasts are not always done their job; when left for a long time in contact with wine (especially white wines), the remains of the yeast cells called *lies* (lees) infuse the wine with proteins that give it more body and a rounder mouthfeel. This process, called *sur lie* (leaving the wine on the lees) or *bâtonnage* (stirring the lees with a stick) is indispensable for the production of Champagne and many sparkling wines, but is also used for the elaboration of many white wines including **Muscadet.**

3. Oxygen

Yeasts are not the only way to convert sugar into alcohol. In absence of oxygen, the yeasts can't do their job, but a special technique called 'carbonic maceration', made famous by Beaujolais uses the natural enzymes contained in the juice to convert sugar into alcohol in absence of oxygen. This too produces Carbon Dioxide, and to happen needs to be made with whole clusters directly closed in a hermetic vat filled with Carbon Dioxide.

Besides Beaujolais, semi-carbonic maceration, a technique that starts with a carbonic maceration finished by a more traditional fermentation is used by the winemakers who want to bring fruit flavours and reduce the tannins. It is very popular in Spain in the Rioja region, but often used when fermenting Carignan in the Languedoc.

4. Carbon dioxide

This gas is what makes the bubbles in sparkling wines. Still wine is fermented in open vats, so the carbon dioxide is released, but to make sparkling wines there are 2 techniques: the rarely used ancestral method which uses the main fermentation of the wine to create bubbles (with lower alcohol levels and gas pressure), and the more common traditional method which uses a second fermentation to create sparkling wines with a higher alcohol level and higher pressure. We will discuss them below.

5. Alcohol

Various yeast cells have different resistance to alcohol levels, and nowadays it's not unusual to find still wines with over 14% abv. As mentioned earlier, adding alcohol during fermentation kills the yeasts and increases the alcohol levels, making it a fortified wine.

So you can see the major parameters a winemaker can adjust, and that's only for the primary fermentation.

Once the alcoholic fermentation is done, a second fermentation can occur: the malo-lactic fermentation (MLF, or "malo"), where the malic acid in the must (a.k.a. the fermenting juice) is converted to lactic acid. All red wines go through this, but for white winemaking it's a choice. Preventing malo results in wines that are tarter because of the malic acid (think green apple) which is well suited for fresh, dry whites, while letting it happens brings buttery notes and a rounder mouthfeel because of the lactic acid (think buttermilk).

This is what makes some Chardonnays (like high-end Bourgogne) "buttery".

————

White, red and rosé winemaking

The goal of white winemaking is to impart as little colour as possible to the wine, so grapes are pressed early to let the clear juice run out and be fermented. In most cases, the goal is to preserve fresh and floral aromas, so many winemakers use a fairly low temperature for fermentation vats (whether in naturally cooled cellars or by using temperature-controlled vats).

In contrast, red winemaking uses the skins and sometimes stems to give the wine the colour and tannins the winemaker is looking for. Sometimes they will opt for a pre-fermentation soak (*macération à froid*), where the grapes are left in contact at fairly cold temperatures to inhibit fermentation but give time for tannins and colour to diffuse into the juice.

Then during fermentation, the skins tend to float at the surface so a variety of techniques can be used to mix juice and skins. *Pigeage* (manually punching down the skins in the juice) is the most gentle extraction method although labor intensive, whereas *Remontage* (pumping the juice over the skins) is automatable but more suited to high extraction, deeply coloured wines. The fastest/harshest method for extraction is called *Délestage* (rack and return) where the entire vat is emptied of its juice, leaving the skins at the bottom, then the must (fermenting juice) is mixed back into the vat.

When making rosé, a winemaker can either use white winemaking technique with a small amount of maceration, or use red wine-making techniques with short maceration time.

The first method, called *vin de presse* (direct press), most commonly used in Provence gives a short maceration time to impart some colour to the must, which tends to give floral aromas with a refreshing acidity. The second method called *saignée* (bleeding) extracts the juice during the fermentation of a red wine, which tends to give more powerful, structured rosés. While it can be used like in Tavel or the Loire as a means of producing rosé, it is also sometimes used as part of red winemaking. By extracting some of the juice/must for rosé, it gives the remaining must a higher content of skins to macerate into, which increases the extraction of colour and tannins; for this reason, saignée rosé coming from appellations that make red wines tends to be just a lower quality by-product of red winemaking.

While most rosé is made using either method, sparkling rosé (including Champagne) is usually made by blending red and white still wines before the second fermentation.

————

Sparkling winemaking

Most sparkling wine is made using the *Méthode Traditionnelle* (traditional method) often called *Méthode Champenoise* in Champagne.

With this technique, still wine (both white and red used in rosé sparkling wine) is made using the normal winemaking technique. Once the wine is made, it is usually blended with the right mix for the appellation, then put bottled along with a mix of sugar and yeast (called *liqueur de tirage*). In the bottle, a second fermentation will occur, trapping the carbon dioxide in the form of bubbles and the yeast cells in the form of lees.

By controlling the mix of sugar and yeast, the winemaker can produce the desired amount of pressure and final alcohol level.

Once the fermentation is done and the wine has remained on its lees for a while (a few months to a few years depending on the appellation), the bottle is quickly opened to evacuate the spent yeasts, a mix of still wine and sugar (called *liqueur de dosage*) is added for the desired amount of final sweetness, and the bottle is closed back with a mushroom-shaped cork for sale.

This technique is what differentiates most French *Crémant* and *Mousseux* from the Italian Prosecco, for which the second fermentation happens in large tanks, resulting in a lower carbon dioxide pressure which leads to larger, flabbier bubbles. A good quality Champagne will have a very fine bubble structure (called *Mousse*) with its minimum of 6 atmospheres of pressure in the bottle.

Another technique to make sparkling wine is the *Méthode Ancestrale* which is only used in a few appellations, and is the original technique for sparkling winemaking. Instead of the 2 fermentations, the ancestral method interrupts the first fermentation by cooling the mixture of partially fermented must and yeast, then bottling it.

Once this mix is bottled, the temperature is raised again and the fermentation finishes. Because of the lack of added sugar, the alcohol levels are lower and since the lees remain in the bottle the wine is usually cloudier.

———

Stainless steel, oak and oxygen

The other choice that a winemaker has to make during this process is whether to preserve the freshness of the fruit or develop more complex flavours. We discussed temperature control, which is very important, but the role of oxygen during the fermentation and especially during aging is also crucial.

Winemaking techniques which tend to avoid oxygen are called reductive, while those who use oxygen are called oxidative.

Reductive techniques enhance the freshness of the fruit, but at the extreme can bring flavours or sulphur (struck match), garlic or rotten eggs. Oxidative techniques enhance the complexity of the wine and bring out dried fruit and nutty flavours, but at the extreme can make wines flat and lifeless.

Reductive winemaking limits the amount of oxygen through the use of stainless steel vats, temperature control and the addition of sulphites. Most white wines, rosés and easy drinking reds tend to be made this way, which bring out the floral notes in white wines and the juiciness of reds and rosés.

Controlled oxidation can yield more complexity and develops aromas that make the best wines incomparable. For this, wooden vats are often used, whether it's large *foudres* or small *barriques*; oak is the primary choice although some regions use walnut and other woods. As wines are aged in oak vats, a very limited amount of oxygen penetrates the wine and develops these complex flavours and a more well rounded body. To mimic the effect of oak aging, some wine makers use a technique called 'micro-oxygenation', basically blowing really small bubbles of air in a stainless steel vat, although this practice is quite controversial. At the extreme end, wines can be left in barrels with some air, like *vin jaune* of Jura where extreme oxidization is a feature, not a bug, very much like Spanish Sherry

That said, oak's role can be more than bringing oxygen to the party. Oak, especially new barrels, impart both flavour and tannins to the wine they contain, and for this reason, many of the high end wines are aged at least partly in new oak. Oak is a family of species, and for the most part French wines use French oak (which imparts more baking spice aromas) although some producers are using some portion of American Oak (which imparts more vanilla/coconut flavours).

Oak is what gives white Bourgogne its power and red Bordeaux its longevity, and with a careful winemaker can elevate a wine from great to sublime. Oak is pretty expensive (especially unused barrels of oak called "new" oak) so it is often used on higher end wines. But old oak is much more widely used and while it does not bring any flavour, it helps with controlled oxygenation and mouthfeel.

PART II

FRENCH WINE REGIONS

6

LOIRE

F resh, light and zesty wines. Lots of whites (Sauvignon Blanc, Chenin Blanc and Muscadet), well regarded sparkling but also reds and rosés (some off-dry) made with Cabernet Franc and Pinot Noir.

Appellations to know:

Sancerre AOC, **Pouilly-Fumé** AOC, **Muscadet** AOC, **Chinon** AOC and **Bourgueil** AOC.

Overview

The Loire valley is located west and slightly south of Paris and it spans a very large area. Because it's in the northern half of France, the climate is fairly cool to grow grapes, but it is moderated by the Loire river and the Atlantic ocean which limits the damage from frost.

Like other cool climate wines, Loire valley wines tend to be fairly high in acidity and lighter bodied, which makes them good pairings for shellfish, fish, salads and lighter fare.

Geography, grapes and styles

Broadly speaking, the Loire valley is usually divided in 3 geographic areas, each grounded by specific grapes and styles of wines: the Upper Loire is dominated by Sauvignon Blanc and Pinot Noir, the Middle Loire by Chenin Blanc and Cabernet Franc, and the Lower Loire by Muscadet.

Upper Loire

Undeniably the most renowned appellations of the Loire valley lie up the river, closer to Champagne and Chablis, and are the most floral expression of French Sauvignon blanc.

Lying on opposite sides of the Loire river, **Sancerre** and **Pouilly-Fumé** are the heavyweights nowadays, but the first village to receive an AOC was **Quincy** and similar wines shine in **Menetou-Salon** and **Reuilly**. All these wines express the herbaceous notes of Sauvignon, but the terroir shines through it. Pouilly-Fumé wines are notorious for their smoky undertones (tip: Fumé means smoky) imparted by the flint they grow on, while Sancerre expresses more minerality.

But red lovers will also find Pinot Noir based wines that show more vibrancy than their **Bourgogne** counterparts. **Sancerre** produces both rosés and reds that hint of cherry with soft tannins, as does **Reuilly**.

Middle Loire (Anjou, Saumur, Touraine)

The middle Loire is the most varied part of the region both in terms of grapes grown but also style of wines. The 2 most important grapes of this area are Chenin blanc and Cabernet Franc.

. . .

Chenin blanc is the base for **Crémant de Loire**, the only French sparkling wine that must be aged longer than Champagne, but is also used for still wines. **Savennières** is the flagship dry white appellation, and due to its high acidity can be aged for many years (the best, hailing from **Coulée de Serrant** and **Roche aux Moines** sometimes peak 20 years after harvest !), but Chenin is used in many other off-dry and sweet wines, like **Coteaux du Layon** and its sister appellations (**Chaume, Quarts de Chaume, Coteaux de l'Aubance, Bonnezeau** and **Anjou Coteaux de la Loire**).

Vouvray is the chameleon of the region as they produce still and sparkling, from dry to sweet Chenin blanc-based wines, as does **Montlouis**. Residual sugar is often not well labeled so expect some level of surprise, unless you know the producer.

Cabernet Franc, often blended with a bit of Cabernet Sauvignon is king near **Chinon** and its neighbour **Bourgueil** where the reds are usually served cool to express their acidity and pair well with poultry but also *rillettes* (a specialty from Tours).

But Cabernet is also the base for many rosés produced in the region, including **Cabernet d'Anjou** (off-dry), **Rosé de Loire** (dry) and **Cabernet de Saumur** (dry). **Rosé d'Anjou**, while it usually contains both Cabernets is primarily based on a local variety called *Grolleau* and is off-dry [1].

Sauvignon Blanc is also well planted, especially moving up the Loire river; some great value can be found in the **Touraine** appellation as well as in the **IGP Val de Loire**

Lower Loire

Sometimes called Pays Nantais (after the city of Nantes), the area closest to the Atlantic ocean is well know for growing Melon Blanc (also known as Melon de Bourgogne or Muscadet) in several appellations which include Muscadet in their names the largest being **Muscadet-Sèvre et Maine**, with also **Muscadet-Coteaux de la Loire**, **Muscadet-Côtes de Grandlieu** and simply **Muscadet AOC**.

Muscadet wines are dry, white wines with high acidity and light body, well known by shellfish lovers around the world (not surprising, the Atlantic coast is a large producer of oysters). To improve the mouthfeel of this grape which can be a bit thin, most producers age Muscadet on the lees, which you will see by the mention *sur lie* on the label (for example **Muscadet-Sèvre et Maine sur lie**).

Of note are the sub-zones of Muscadet-Sèvre et Maine which must be aged on the lees for an even longer time: **Château-Thébaud, Clisson, Gorges, Goulaine, Monnières – Saint-Fiacre, Mouzillon – Tillières** and **Le Pallet**. Unfortunately, for those the label will mention the zone name but not *sur lie* despite the longer time spent on the lees.

You may also find on the shelves **Gros Plant du Pays Nantais**, a local, grassy dry white made with *Folle Blanche* (a grape used to make brandy). Look for *sur lie* versions as they tend to offset the natural bitterness of the grape.

---

1. For Loire rosés, if it has 'Anjou' in the name it's probably off-dry, if not it's probably dry

7

CHAMPAGNE

C elebrate with bubbles. The blend of Chardonnay, Pinot Noir and Pinot Meunier grows on a unique soil and develops complex flavours during aging. Yes it's expensive, but the taste is unmatched in the word of sparkling wines.

Appellations to know:

Champagne AOC, *Millésimé, Blanc de Blanc*

Overview

Champagne is all about bubbles. They make sparkling wine all over the world, even in other French regions, so why is Champagne so special ? The soil, the blend of grapes, as well as the winemaking technique all combine into a wine that is unmatched anywhere in the world.

Geography, grapes and styles

The Champagne region is situated east of Paris, around the town of Reims (where Clovis, first king of France was crowned). It's pretty much as far north as grapes can grow in France, which makes it hard for grapes to fully ripen and keeps them freshly acidic.

There are only 3 grapes allowed in **Champagne:** Chardonnay, Pinot Noir and Pinot Meunier (think of it as a close cousin of Pinot Noir). And even though these grapes can be grown in many places, Champagne soil is unique in the world because of the combination of chalk and marl that was formed 150 million years ago when the region was at the edge of the sea; this soil gives a particular taste to the grapes that is unmatched.

The wine is made using the traditional method, where the winemaker takes still wine (likely a blend of wines) and mixes it in a bottle with yeast and sugar, so that the combination will create a gas (carbon dioxide) responsible for the formation of bubbles.

Champagne bottles must be aged on their lees (the remains of spent yeast cells) which smoothes the mouthfeel and gives toasted bread/brioche notes to the wine. After this long period of aging, the lees are removed (disgorging), and the Champagne is then finished by adding a mix of wine and sugar to adjust the sweetness level and bottled with a cork in its final bottle.

Types of Champagne

Given the fact that the region is so northerly and the weather affects the grape growing season probably even more than anywhere else, Champagne has some very unusual rules when it comes to winemaking.

The first is that most Champagne is a blend of multiple years. By reserving a sizeable portion of the wine year after year and blending the prior years into the current year's wine, the Champagne houses can create a blend that is consistent year after year and does not suffer from vintage variations. It's commonly referred to as "non-vintage" and is the most common type of Champagne.

The second is that *Champagne Rosé* is actually made from mixing red and white wines before the second fermentation.

Millésimé (vintage) Champagne is only made in excellent years when grapes are sufficiently ripe and is usually more expensive, but tends to be an improvement over the usual house blend.

There are also two labels you may encounter: *Blanc de Blanc* and *Blanc de Noir*.

- *Blanc de Blanc* means that instead of the usual Champagne blend of 3 grapes, this is made with 100% Chardonnay; depending on the place it was grown it can range from fine and delicate to rich and powerful.
- *Blanc de Noir* means that it's only made out of Pinot (Noir or Meunier). While they are white sparkling wines, they express bit more tannins and more fruity notes.

We discussed the **Champagne** AOC, but still wine is also produced, most of it going in Champagne production but some sold as is under the **Coteaux Champenois** appellation. You can try it out of curiosity, but it's unlikely to blow your mind.

Sweetness level

The other very important aspect of Champagne is the *liqueur de dosage* which is the wine/sugar blend that is added right prior to the final bottling. Champagne is very acidic, so some amount of sugar will balance it out. While sweeter styles of Champagne were more popular in the past, today the most common will be Brut which is fairly dry. The poorly named *Sec* is not dry, but rather off-dry, while Brut Nature (without any added sugar) tends to be almost sour and thin, save for the exceptional warm vintage.

Here are all the sweetness levels, in order from the driest to the sweetest:

---

brut nature, extra brut, brut, extra sec, sec, demi sec, doux

(no sugar, bone dry, dry, off-dry, semi-sweet, sweet, very sweet)

Champagne houses

Most Champagne wine is produced by Champagne Houses which buy most of the grapes they bottle from growers (although they also grow some themselves).

The Champagne Houses are the brands of Champagne and most of them have 2 tiers of brands: the house brand and the *tête de cuvée* which is their flagship brand, offering their best product.

Here are some famous Champagne house, followed by their Tête de cuvée:

- Moët & Chandon: Dom Pérignon
- Veuve Cliquot: La Grande Dame
- Roederer: Cristal
- Taittinger: Comtes de Champagne
- Laurent Perrier: Grand Siècle
- Mumm: Grande Cuvée de Mumm
- Gosset: Celebris

But in recent years, growers/winemakers have started to grow in importance and give some serious competition to the best Champagne houses. But if you are looking at a few bottles, how do you know whether you are dealing with a grower or a house ?

There is a 2-letter code on every champagne bottle somewhere on the label; sometimes it's hard to find but it has to be there by law.

Here is what the codes mean:

- NM (*Négociant-Manipulant*): A producer that incorporates grapes from other growers. Most Champagne houses are NM
- RM (*Récoltant-Manipulant*): A producer who only makes wines with grapes they grow.
- RC (*Récoltant-Coopérateur*): A producer who is part of a cooperative, but resells the wines under their own name.
- SR (*Société de Récoltants*): A group of growers who sell the wines under a joint name
- CM (*Coopérative de Manipulation*): A co-operative cellar that makes wines from grapes grown by its members
- MA (*Marque Auxiliaire*) A private label used by restaurants, wine stores, supermarkets, etc... It could be made by anyone of the above
- ND (*Négociant-Distributeur*) Used for wine buyers who buy wines from any above and resells them under their own brand.

So look for NM (Champagne house) or RM (grower-producer) Champagnes. RC/SR and CM are cooperatives of varying quality, and with MA/ND you really need to trust the reseller because you don't know who made it.

Cellaring

Champagne is meant to be drunk not long after final bottling (definitely within 10 years, ideally before 5), because the gas (under 6 bars of pressure) slowly escapes from the bottle through the cork. So if you buy an old Champagne you are likely going to be disappointed. More and more, good producers will put the disgorging date or will market their wines as 'recently disgorged' for those older Champagnes that are still fresh.

Last, unlike other wines, Champagne is actually aged in standard sized bottles, so if you buy a magnum or larger of Champagne it will have been mixed from 2 or more standard size bottles after disgorging, so save your money and buy 2 bottles instead.

8

ALSACE

G erman influences with French finesse. Very distinctive white wines (Riesling, Gewurztraminer, Pinot Gris) in an elongated bottle called *flute.*

Appellations to know:

Alsace AOC, **Alsace Grand Cru** AOC, **Crémant d'Alsace** AOC

Overview

Alsace wine is recognizable by 2 things: long, thin, german-style bottles called *flutes* and the label names the grape in the bottle (and there is usually one). And unlike many other regions of France, most wine is made with a single variety and labelled as such.

Like neighbouring Germany, it's a cool climate region that is mostly focused mostly on making white wine (both still and sparkling). Riesling, Gewürztraminer, Pinot Gris and Muscat are the 'noble' varieties of Alsace, although Pinot Noir is used to craft a very light red wine that is rarely seen outside of the region.

Geography, grapes and styles

Alsace has one regional appellation, with 13 villages that can append their names to the designation, and 51 Grand Crus.

Alsace quality pyramid

Alsace AOC

Alsace is located on the east side of France, on the east side of the Vosges Mountain in the slopes of the Rhine valley, right by the German border. The Vosges block the rain coming from the west, making Alsace an unusually warm and dry place given its latitude. The **Alsace** AOC covers the entire region, the others AOC are for sub-zones or specific production methods.

Alsace wine growers categorize 5 white grapes as "noble": Riesling, Pinot Gris, Gewurztraminer and the 2 Muscats (Blanc & Ottonel). But Sylvaner, Chasselas and Pinot Blanc as well as Pinot Noir and a few others are grown as well, mostly for sparkling wine production. Most wines are meant to be drunk fairly young (within 5 years), although good Riesling can last decades when properly cellared.

While Alsace AOC can be used all over the region, 13 villages can add their names to the appellation because of the higher standards of production: **Bergheim, Blienschwiller, Coteaux du Haut-Koenigsbourg, Côtes de Barr, Côte de Rouffach, Klevener de Heiligenstein, Ottrott, Rodern, Saint-Hippolyte, Scherwiller, Vallée Noble, Val Saint Grégoire** and **Wolxheim.**

Riesling is the king of Alsace, but unlike its german counterparts it is usually finished dry. Aromas of peach and apricot are common, although aged riesling develop notes of petrol, and it pairs wonderfully with quiche, sauerkraut and *flammekuche* (a thin pizza dough topped with cream, onion and bacon).

Gewurztraminer is a very aromatic grape, with lychee or grape notes, and it especially suited to late harvesting.

Pinot Gris, while technically the same grape as the Italian Pinot Grigio, tends to be finished with a smidge of residual sugar which gives it more body.

There is a small production of red wine made with Pinot Noir that is very light in colour, almost like a dark rosé, but most of it is drunk locally.

Alsace Grand Cru AOC

There are 51 *Grand Cru* in Alsace, which are designated vineyard that have exceptional characteristics. Each ones have stricter production rules than the Alsace AOC and only allow a single noble grape in the bottle.

The only exceptions are **Alternberg de Bergheim** which can be a Riesling-based blend, **Kaefferkopf** which can be a Gewurztraminer-based blend and **Zotzenberg** which allows Sylvaner.

The bottles will be labeled with the cru name, Alsace, Grand Cru and the grape in various order, for example **Rangen Riesling - Alsace Grand Cru AOC** or **Schoenenbourg Grand Cru d'Alsace - Riesling**. Some other notable grand crus are **Vorbourg, Hengst, Schlossberg, Geisberg** and **Muenchberg**.

Sweet wines

Semi-sweet wines will be labeled *Vendanges Tardives* (late harvest) and will be made with hand harvested noble varieties.

Sweet wines are labeled *Sélection de Grains Nobles* (sometimes abbreviated as SGN) which are also based on noble varieties, but have to be made from individually handpicked berries affected by botrytis (similar to the German *Beerenauslese* or *Trockenbeerenauslese*).

Blends of Alsace AOC

Over 80% of wine produced in Alsace is made with a single grape in the bottle. Most blends are used in **Crémant d'Alsace**, a sparkling wine made with the traditional method, handpicked and whole cluster pressed which is usually a Pinot Blanc based blend.

However, there are 2 blended wines in the Alsace AOC of note: *Gentil* and *Edelzwicker*. Gentil is made with over 50% of noble grapes and can be a simple, versatile dry white wine. In contrast, there are little limitations on the grapes that can be used for Edelzwicker which seems to be designed as a way to use the bottom of the barrels.

9

JURA, SAVOIE & BUGEY

Distinctive grapes and winemaking techniques for these high altitude wines.

Appellations to know:

Arbois AOC, **Côtes du Jura** AOC, **Savoie** AOC, **Bugey** AOC, *Vin Jaune*

Overview

Both Savoie and Jura are located on the east side of France near the Swiss border.

The Jura wine region sits in between Bourgogne and Switzerland, on the slopes of the Jura mountains at the foothills the Alps. It's most famous for its *Vin Jaune* (a deeply oxidized white wine similar in style to Sherry), but crafts some unique wines with local grapes.

. . .

The Savoie wine region is nestled in the Alps, around and a bit further South of Geneva lake, which provides a temperature buffer against the cold of the mountains. Still, it's a cool climate region that specializes in light bodied, high acidity wines with unique grapes.

Bugey is a closer to the Rhône river, and has recently been awarded its own AOC.

Geography, grapes and styles

Vin Jaune, Vin de Paille and Macvin du Jura

Vin Jaune is a unique style of wine that is made in Jura with the Savagnin Blanc grape. After fermentation, the wine is stored for over 6 years in wooden casks with a heavy amount of air space, which causes the wine to oxidize in a controlled fashion (like Sherry), giving it distinct whiff of aldehydes (think Pine-Sol floor cleaner).

This style of wine is sold in 620ml bottles (as a nod to the wine that evaporates during the maturing period) and can be found in **Arbois**, l'Étoile, **Château-Chalon** and **Côtes du Jura**.

Vin de Paille (straw wine) is a style that can be found in Jura in the same AOCs as vin jaune. For this, grapes (Chardonnay, Poulsard and/or Savagnin) are left to dry on straw mats after harvest to concentrate the sugars before fermentation. The resulting wine is white, naturally sweet and aged for over 3 years. Like Vin Jaune, these wines are very suitable for long term cellaring.

Macvin du Jura is a blend of grape alcohol and unfermented juice aged for at least a year. It's usually white (although red versions exist) with a final alcohol level of around 20%.

Local red varieties

There are two red grapes are distinctively grown in Jura: Poulsard (sometimes named Ploussard) and Trousseau, and can mostly be found in the **Arbois** AOC and **Côtes du Jura** AOC. Many producers use organic or low touch methods in the production of wine made with these varieties. While Poulsard makes lightly coloured reds and is often vinified into a white wine named *vin gris* (grey wine), Trousseau's concentration is deeper.

Not to be left out, Savoie grows Mondeuse, which makes medium-low alcohol red wines that are refreshingly bright. It's sold under the **Savoie** AOC, and can be either made with a single grape or blended with Gamay or Pinot Noir. Red Savoie AOC has 5 *Cru* villages (**Arbin, Chautagne, Chignin, Jongieux** and **St. Jean de la Porte**).

Refreshing white & sparkling wines

While reds are produced in Savoie, most of **Savoie** AOC is white, made in a dry, light style. Jacquère is a uniquely Savoyard grape that pairs wonderfully with melted cheese dishes (fondue, raclette and the like). 14 'Cru' villages are allowed to put their names on white Savoie AOC, **Apremont, Chautagne, Chignin** and **Jongieux** amongst them, where the wines must contain at least 80% Jacquère.

Another typical grape from Savoie is Altesse, mostly sold as **Roussette de Savoie** AOC. Fuller-bodied and spicier than Jacquère, this refreshing white wine is a treat. **Roussette du Bugey** AOC follows the same template. **Seyssel** AOC still wines are based on Altesse, although it was better known for its sparkling wines based on Molette (another local grape).

Bugey AOC is a pink sparkling wine made with Gamay using the ancestral method (called *Méthode Cerdon* from the name of the village it is produced in)

Outside of Vin Jaune and other specialties, Jura's whites are dominated by Chardonnay and provide an alternative to higher priced white Bourgogne.

10

BOURGOGNE

BURGUNDY

W hites are made with Chardonnay (with or without oak), and reds with Pinot Noir. But more than the grape, the terroir shines through the best wines, especially in the *Grand Crus* and *Premier Crus*

Appellations to know:

Bourgogne AOC, Chablis AOC, Macon AOC, Côte-de-Nuits Villages AOC, Côte-de-Beaune Villages AOC, *villages, grand crus, premier crus.*

Overview

On the surface, Bourgogne is one of the simplest wine regions to understand. Almost all of the reds produced there are made with 100% Pinot Noir. Whites are mostly made with 100% Chardonnay with one nuance: around Chablis it's made without the influence of oak to create a lean, mineral dry white wine, but further south, in the

Côte d'Or, Côte Chalonnaise and Mâconnais, oak is more liberally used, especially on higher end wines.

Simple, right ?

Well, what makes Bourgogne special is that the grape in the bottle only tells half of the story. Both Chardonnay and Pinot Noir are experts at expressing terroir, meaning that depending on where it is grown, the same grape will taste very differently once made into wine. So unsurprisingly, there are over 100 appellations for Bourgogne only, most of them not even mentioning Bourgogne on the label.

Thankfully, Bourgogne has introduced a classification system which helps set expectations of the quality of the wine.

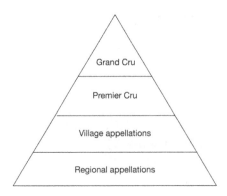

Quality pyramid of Bourgogne

Grand Cru is the top echelon of the quality pyramid, accounting for around 2% of the wine volume. Each grand cru (there are 33 of them) has their own appellation, and these wines are made from grapes grown in small parcels, many of them delineated by monks in the middle ages.

Second on the scale, the *Premier Cru* (roughly 10% of the production) parcels are the best parcels in villages, and labelled under their village's AOC.

Then, comes the village AOCs (there are 44 of them) where wines can be made from grapes grown anywhere around the named village.

Last are the 24 regional AOC (which usually contain Bourgogne in the name) which are blends of grapes grown anywhere in the region.

Confusingly, many villages that have a grand cru added the name of it to the village name, for example the village of Gevrey-Chambertin includes the name of its grand cru **Chambertin**. But the bottles will be labeled with *Grand Cru* or *Premier Cru* if they come from there, so in doubt look for this on the label.

In Bourgogne, especially in the Côte d'Or the grand cru are located for the most part in the middle of the slope. The premier crus tend to be located just above or below, while the *Hautes Côtes* are at the top of the hills, and the remainder of the villages appellations is at the bottom, where the soil is more fertile, yielding more volume with less flavour concentration.

Geography and wine styles

If the Chablis region focuses mostly on whites wines, the rest of Bourgogne is more of a gradient, where Pinot Noir is the most thought after in the Côte de Nuits, and the importance of Chardonnay grows as you travel south towards Mâcon.

Côte d'Or

This is the heart of Burgundy. Outside of the one **Chablis Grand Cru**, all of Bourgogne's Grand Crus are located in this area, which is usually further divided in two: the Côte de Nuits (around the town of Nuit-Saint-Georges) where most grand crus are reds, and the Côte de Beaune (around the town of Beaune) where most of the grand crus are white. Of course, for both premier cru and village wines, both reds and whites are produced. This is where the best Bourgogne is produced and overall the quality of the wines produced here is greater than in the other parts of Bourgogne.

Côte de Nuits

The grand crus are all located in the villages of **Gevrey-Chambertin, Morey-Saint-Denis, Chambolle-Musigny, Vougeot** and **Vosne-Romanée.**

Some of the most famous grand crus include **Chambertin, Clos de Bèze, Bonne Mares, Clos de Vougeot, Romanée-Conti, Grands Échezaux. Musigny** is the only Grand Cru in the Côte de Nuits that allows white wine production, even though the bulk of Musigny is red.

Not to be left out, **Fixin, Marsannay** (known for its rosé) and of course **Nuits-Saint-George** produce high quality village wines and premier crus.

Côtes de Nuits-Villages (mostly red) is made with grapes coming from villages in the middle of the slopes, whereas **Hautes Côtes de Nuits** is reserved for villages at the top of the hill.

Côte de Beaune

The grand crus are all concentrated in the villages of **Ladoix (Ladoix-Serrigny), Aloxe-Corton, Pernand-Vergelesse, Puligny-Montrachet** and **Chassagne-Montrachet.** Most grand crus are exclusively white, including **Charlemagne, Corton-Charlemagne, Montrachet** and

Bâtard-Montrachet; **Corton** is the only grand cru in Côte de Beaune that allows red wine production.

Beaune, Pommard, Volnay, Maranges and **Santenay** are well regarded villages for red wine production, while **Meursault, Saint-Romain, Saint-Aubin** shine for their whites.

Like in Côte de Nuits, **Côtes de Beaune-Villages** (mostly red) is made with grapes coming from villages in the middle of the slopes, whereas **Hautes Côtes de Beaune** is reserved for villages at the top of the hill.

Côte Chalonnaise & Mâconnais

Past the Côte d'Or, the balance of whites increases as you travel south.

Côte Chalonnaise

Mercurey is the anchor village of the Chalonnais and with its 32 premier crus vineyards produces well rounded but firmly acidic reds, but **Givry** and **Rully** have many premier crus that should not be left behind.

Montagny is a well regarded white-only appellation whose racy wines often bring mineral notes with a hint of spice.

Also of note, **Bouzeron**, the only white village appellation in southern Bourgogne that is made with 100% Aligoté rather than Chardonnay.

Mâconnais

While Pinot Noir is grown in the Mâconnais, most of the production feeds the generic Bourgogne regional appellations and red **Mâcon** AOC. The main grape there is Chardonnay, and while Mâcon AOC and the various **Mâcon-Villages** AOC dominate the production, the best expression of it is **Pouilly-Fuissé** and its neighbours **Pouilly-Loché** and **Pouilly-Vinzelles**.

For uncomplicated wines, look for **Lugny, Saint-Véran** and **Viré-Clessé** which still deliver the style of Bourgogne Chardonnay although in a less refined way.

Chablis

Last thing of note, the vineyards of Chablis are located at much higher latitudes than the rest of Bourgogne, making it closer to the Loire valley or even Champagne (which which it shares a soil).

Chablis appellations

In contrast with the often rich expression of Chardonnay that Southern Bourgogne produces, Chablis has forged a reputation for making very high quality, lean and quite often mineral wines. The soil there is reminiscent of Champagne with old marine deposits in limestone.

This 100% Chardonnay is mostly fermented in stainless steel, although some producers are using old oak barrels to impart a roundness without adding oak flavours.

There are 4 'levels' of Chablis:

- **Chablis Grand Cru** (further subdivided in 7 *climats* named **Blanchot, Bougros, Les Clos, Grenouilles, Les Preuses, Valmur** and **Vaudésir**) is the purest expression of Chablis. Long-lived, it benefits from bottle aging (10 years) and the best examples stay fresh for decades.

- **Chablis Premier Cru** (there are 40 named crus) is the next level down. While there is some variation, this is probably where the best value in Chablis wine can be found. The wines should be cellared for a few years before enjoying.

- **Chablis AOC**: can be even more uneven than the Premier Crus, although is consistently shows a minerality and leanness that pairs wonderfully with shellfish.

- **Petit Chablis AOC**: grown in the plains, this wine is mostly forgettable and is a weak shadow of Chablis.

Other wines of the Grand Auxerrois

The other wines grown in the area are closer in style to Upper Loire valley wines. **Saint-Bris** is notable for being the only white Bourgogne made with 100% Sauvignon Blanc, and some Pinot Noir-based red wine is produced in **Irancy** and **Coulanges-La-Vineuse** which are very light in style.

Regional appellations

The bulk of Bourgogne wine is sold under the **Bourgogne AOC**, and if not based on Chardonnay or Pinot Noir will be labelled as such. For example the uncomplicated white **Bourgogne Aligoté** is based on Aligoté, or the red **Bourgogne Gamay** will be based on Gamay.

Bourgogne Passe-Tout-Grains and **Coteaux Bourguignons** (formerly known as **Bourgogne Grand Ordinaire**) are inexpensive blends of the locally grown grapes, usually Pinot Noir and Gamay and is not really representative of the rest of Bourgogne wines, but provide low end table wine.

Bourgogne-Côte d'Or is a regional appellation which covers all of the Côte d'Or, and the wines will be Chardonnay or Pinot Noir based and are a definite step up from the regular Bourgogne AOC.

Last, **Crémant de Bourgogne** is a Pinot / Chardonnay sparkling wine which can be reminiscent of Champagne.

11

BEAUJOLAIS

E minently drinkable reds, where Gamay can be made into wine that can go from candy flavoured to delightfully complex.

Appellations to know:

Beaujolais AOC, **Beaujolais-Villages** AOC, **Brouilly** AOC, **Morgon** AOC, **Moulin-A-Vent** AOC, **Fleurie** AOC.

Overview

Beaujolais used to be part of Bourgogne before the French revolution, and some villages in Beaujolais are still allowed to grow grapes sold as Bourgogne. But Beaujolais has developed into a style that is too distinct from Bourgogne that it deserves to be considered on its own.

While some white Beaujolais made with Chardonnay is produced, the region distinguishes itself by making its reds from Gamay, and the use of carbonic maceration. This fermentation technique uses enzymes contained in the grapes rather than yeasts to convert the sugar into alcohol, and preserves juicy fruit flavours that would otherwise be more muted by a traditional fermentation.

Quickly fermented wines sold in large volumes in late November after harvest under the **Beaujolais Nouveau** appellation have without a doubt been a successful marketing strategy in the late 20th century, but this cheap, candy flavoured wine as fallen out of favour with many wine lovers.

But the rise and fall of Beaujolais Nouveau should not cast a shadow over the wines that the region produces. **Beaujolais** and its better brother **Beaujolais-Village** are very versatile every day wines, and the 10 Crus of Beaujolais offer an expression of terroir that holds themselves on par with some of Bourgogne's village wines.

Geography, grapes and styles

Like in Bourgogne and Alsace, there is a quality pyramid in Beaujolais:

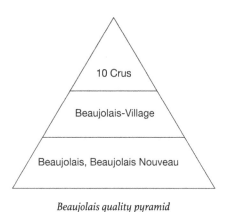

Beaujolais quality pyramid

Beaujolais and Beaujolais-Villages

This wine is made mostly from grapes grown in the southern part of the Beaujolais region. Fruit-forward, fairly high acidity and low tannins is a winning combination for drinkability. It can easily be paired with many dishes and for this reason is the classic 'bistro' wine.

While **Beaujolais** is often the cheapest offering, **Beaujolais-Villages** often provides better value as its flavours are more concentrated, and brings slightly more tannins which improves its structure. Both are meant to be enjoyed within a few years of harvest.

The Beaujolais Crus

Ten villages, all situated in the northern part of Beaujolais have their own appellations. They have some aging potential, and as they age bring characteristics resembling the Pinot Noir-based Bourgogne wines. Wines falling under these Cru AOC must be hand harvested and have much lower yields that regular Beaujolais.

Morgon is well regarded for its expression of terroir and rich cherry flavours.

Moulin-à-Vents (along with its neighbour **Chénas**) is the Beaujolais cru with the most potential for aging (up to 10 years for the best example), bringing slightly more tannins and becoming more pinot-like as it ages.

Juliénas is the most full-bodied cru of Beaujolais, while **Fleurie** makes lighter, more floral wines and in the best years can rival Moulin-à-Vents.

Chiroubles is delicate, and its higher altitude means that it fares better in warm vintages.

Brouilly is the largest cru and the southernmost, and can be quite varied. **Côte de Brouilly** a dedicated appellation fully enclosed in Brouilly AOC.

Saint-Amour, the northernmost cru make both young drinkable wines as well as some that are a bit more tannic and age worthy.

Most crus can add up to 15% of Pinot Noir, Pinot Gris and others to the base of Gamay, but **Régnié** (the newest cru) is 100% Gamay, and offers a generally good consistency.

12

RHÔNE

B old, spicy red wines based on the trinity of Grenache-Syrah and
Mourvèdre, ideal for a barbecue or a summer get-together.

Appellations to know:

Côtes Du Rhône AOC, Châteauneuf-du-Pape AOC, Crozes-
Hermitage AOC, Côte-Rotie AOC, Condrieu AOC

Overview

The Rhône valley lies south of Bourgogne and Beaujolais, and is
where Syrah makes its boldest appearance in French wines. If **Côtes
du Rhône** is its oldest named wine and spans most of the region,
looking closer the region is really split in 2 parts separated by some of
the largest french fruit orchards: the Northern Rhône (*Rhône septen-
trional*) and Southern Rhône (*Rhône méridional*).

.   .   .

If Syrah is the common thread between red wines of the Rhône, the Northern Rhône appellations tend to use it alone, whereas the Southern Rhône appellations, including Côtes du Rhône, blend it with Grenache and Mourvèdre in a blend commonly called "Rhône blend" or GSM (Grenache-Syrah-Mourvèdre).

While the vast majority of wine produced in the region is red, white Rhône wines are usually a blend of Marsanne and Roussanne, but Viognier and Clairette make distinctive appearances.

Geography, grapes and styles

As in Alsace and Bourgogne, there is a quality pyramid in Rhône.

Rhône quality pyramid

Côtes du Rhône and Southern Rhône Crus

The vast majority of production goes towards making red Côtes du Rhône (CDR) and its associated appellations. The base of CDR is Grenache, with Syrah and Mourvèdre as usual blending partners but over 10 grapes are allowed.

. . .

Chateauneuf-du-Pape AOC is certainly the flagship appellation for this style of wine, but like in other areas, there is a quality pyramid you should understand.

At the bottom, **Côtes Du Rhône** AOC where the blending formula is based on percentage of plantings, not percentage of grapes in the bottle. This is why there is so much variation in CDR and they can be disappointing.

A step above CDR, **Côtes Du Rhône Villages** AOC mandates percentages in the actual blend, so will be more consistent. These reds are medium to full bodied and well structured, usually fairly high in alcohol, with both red and dried fruit flavours from the Grenache, blue fruits and peppery aromas from the Syrah and animal notes from the Mourvèdre.

17 Villages can append their name to Côtes du Rhône Villages AOC and tend to bring distinctive characteristics to the glass.

Last, at the top of the pyramid you can find the Rhône Crus. **Chateauneuf-du-Pape** makes full bodied, fleshy reds with ripe tannins. **Gigondas** and **Vinsobres** tend to bring a fresher acidity, while **Vacqueyras, Rasteau sec** and **Lirac** bring denser, meatier notes. The newest cru **Cairanne** is a reliable producer of good value wines.

While reds dominate the picture, some white CDR is produced (based on a Marsanne-Roussanne blend), but rosé has a standout appellation in **Tavel**: here, rosé is made from the *saignée* method, and is deeply concentrated for the pleasure of red wine lovers who want to venture on the rosé side.

. . .

Last, although Rasteau now produces this dry CDR-style wine (labelled *Sec*), it has been historically well known for its *Vin Doux Naturel* (sweet fortified wine) production primarily made with Grenache labelled **Rasteau AOC** (without the word *sec*), as is **Muscat de Beaumes de Venise** with its Muscat blanc-based VDN.

Northern Rhône Crus

Reds in the Northern Rhône are mostly Syrah, although some appellations include some white grapes to enhance the floral aromas, including Viognier or Marsanne and Roussanne.

Côte-Rôtie is probably the famous cru of Rhône, where Viognier is co-planted and co-fermented with Syrah to craft a powerful red that gives distinctive notes of white pepper and cardamom.

Crozes-Hermitage is the largest of the Northern Rhône Crus and with **Hermitage** the only two on the left bank of the Rhône.

Saint-Joseph and **Cornas** round up the northern crus focused on reds.

The flagship of white wines is **Condrieu** and it's fully enclosed sister appellation **Château-Grillet**, which stand out as the best expression of Viognier that French wine has to offer. But the Marsanne-Roussane blend of Hermitage, Crozes-Hermitages and Saint-Joseph can be delightful.

Last, **Saint-Peray** makes both still and sparkling whites with the Marsanne-Roussanne blend that taste more floral and citrusy than its neighbours.

. . .

One thing of note is that Northern Rhône is sightly cooler than Southern Rhône and more susceptible to vintage variation, although top producers usually provide a consist quality despite this.

Other Rhône appellations

There are many other appellations, including **Ventoux, Costières de Nimes, Lubéron, Côtes du Vivarais** and **Grignan-lès-Adhémar** which all make reds, rosés and whites in the same style as CDR.

Also of note, **Clairette de Die** is a refreshing Clairette-based sparkling wine that you may also find on the shelves.

13

PROVENCE & CORSE

D ry, refreshing rosé for these hot summers, but also Italian varieties create interesting whites and reds.

Appellations to know:

Côtes de Provence AOC, **Bandol** AOC, **Cassis** AOC, **Patrimonio** AOC, **Vin de Corse** AOC

Overview

Provence is the only wine region in the worlds that focuses on rosé, and sets the bar for perfumed, refreshingly dry rosé wine. Unlike the very extracted rosés from some other regions, Provence rosé is often very light in colour and high in floral aromas.

But Provence also crafts some very distinctive whites from Clairette and Vermentino (called Rolle) and reds, like Corsica where Italian varieties (Sangiovese and Sciacarello) complete the panel of flavours.

Geography, grapes and styles

Provence rosé

Even though the base blend is similar to Rhône valley reds (Grenache, Syrah, Mourvèdre, but also Cinsault and Tibouren), unlike **Tavel**, most of the rosé made in Provence is made using the direct press method. The grapes are picked fairly early to preserve their acidity and after pressing the really short (or inexistent) maceration enhances the floral aromas of the grapes but imparts very little colour to the wine, making most Provence rosé really light pink, almost grey-pink. But these lighter in alcohol wines (11 to 12% abv usually) are a welcome refreshment for sunny summers.

Oh, and don't think of drinking an old bottle of rosé, they are meant to be consumed within a year after harvest after which they lose the freshness that makes them special.

Most of the wine is labelled under the **Côtes de Provence** AOC, with 4 sub-zones (**Sainte-Victoire, Fréjus, La Londe** and **Pierrefeu**) that can be added on the label. Some estates are allowed to use the *Cru classé* designation. Unlike the other appellations, **Coteaux d'Aix-en-Provence** can include Cabernet Sauvignon.

Coteaux Varois en Provence is cooler and usually produces even more aromatic wines. **Les Baux de Provence** , while it produces rosé, actually produces more red wine and is known for its strong proportion of organic and biodynamic vineyards.

Provence reds and whites

Palette produces more red and white than rosé, as does **Coteaux de Pierrevert** but the most distinctive appellation is without a doubt **Bandol.**

The reds of Bandol AOC are made with mostly Mourvèdre, with some Grenache and Cinsault, giving them a really dark, intense colour, with ripe tannins and strong animal flavours that develop with age. By law it must be aged for 18 months in oak, and will need a few more years in bottle to be enjoyed. Many start peaking after 10 years. Rosés follow a similar blend formula, and can be much more heavy than other Provence rosés.

Cassis stands out as an appellation dominated by its white wine production, with a Marsanne & Clairette-based blend.

Corse

If some Italian grapes like Rolle (Vermentino) and Tibouren (Rossesse de Dolceacqua) are planted in Provence, Corsica is where their proportion outgrows traditional French varieties.

Sangiovese (called Niellucciu in Corse) is **Patrimonio** AOC's answer to Tuscany's Chianti. The bulk of AOC wine falls under the **Vin de Corse** AOC (or **Corse AOC**)but look for one of the 5 sub-zones for more typical wines. Mamollo (called Sciaccarellu) is usually dominant in the sub-zones of **Calvi, Sartène, Figari** and **Porto-Vecchio.** For white wines, look for the sub-zone of **Coteaux du Cap Corse** which produces crisp, dry wines from Vermentino (called Vermentinu).

. . .

While most of Vin de Corse red is a blend of Niellucciu, Sciaccarellu and Grenache with other grapes, a younger generation of wine-makers is redeveloping a market for indigenous varieties, often sold under the **Ile de Beauté IGP.**

Last but not least, **Muscat du Cap Corse** AOC, a Muscat-based vin doux naturel is also produced around the town of Patrimonio.

14

LANGUEDOC & ROUSSILLON

A large supplier of wine, Languedoc has perfected the Rhône blend and the Bordeaux techniques to craft excellent wines.

Appellations to know:

Vin de Pays d'Oc, Languedoc AOC, Côtes du Roussillon AOC, Faugères AOC, Blanquette de Limoux AOC

Overview

The South of France has a long standing reputation for producing large volumes of wine, and to this day the **IGP Pays d'Oc** remains France's biggest wine export. But in the last decades, the quality of the wines produced in Languedoc-Roussillon has raised dramatically, making the region a great source for value wine.

While the coastal part of Languedoc follows in the footsteps of the Rhône Valley with a Grenache Syrah Mourvèdre blend often augmented with Carignan and Cinsault, Carignan's importance grows as you get closer to Spain into Roussillon. But Languedoc also extends inland into the SouthWest part of the country, where Bordeaux grapes (Merlot, Cabernet Sauvignon) get introduced in the blend.

But Languedoc-Roussillon is also the home of several *vin doux naturels*, whether based on Muscat or Grenache as well as some refreshing whites and sparkling wines. Yet by far, the production is dominated by varietal IGP wine produced by cooperatives that is meant to be easy drinking, inexpensive every day wine.

Geography, grapes and styles

The **Languedoc** AOC (formerly **Coteaux du Languedoc** AOC) covers the entire territory of Languedoc-Roussillon, and must be blends of at least 2 varieties. For reds, Grenache (and its local cousin Lledoner Pelut), Syrah and Mourvèdre must be at least 50% of the blend while Carignan and Cinsault cannot be over 40%. For whites, Bourboulenc, Grenache blanc, Marsanne, Roussanne, Vermentino, Clairette and Picpoul can be used.

Because of this large area where Languedoc AOC wine can be produced, there is quite a bit of variation; look for wines with an added mention of an area: **Cabrières, Grés de Montpellier, La Méjanelle, Montpeyroux, Pézenas, Quatourze, Saint-Christol, Saint-Drézéry, Saint-Georges-d'Orques, Saint-Saturnin** and **Sommières.**

Coastal Languedoc

Saint-Chinian is where Carignan's share of the red blend increases, especially in the sub-zones of **Berlou** and **Roquebrun**. That said, the white wines produces there have long been recognized for their finesse.

Faugères are crafted in a similar style but is an organic and biodynamic stronghold where many producers make their own wine and coops are less important. This is unlike **Fitou**, which was the first AOC to be awarded in Languedoc.

Many of the best areas of Languedoc AOC have been granted their own appellations in the recent years. **La Clape, Pic Saint-Loup, Terrasses du Larzac** provide excellent renditions of what Languedoc AOC has to offer.

Picpoul de Pinet, a refreshing white wine from near Sète is Languedoc's answer to Muscadet, a perfect pairing for the local Bouzigues oysters. **Clairette du Languedoc** is also a light white wine but its production is much smaller.

Atlantic corridor

If **Corbières** (especially in the **Boutenac** zone) ramps up the Carignan in the GSM blend, **Minervois** (even more so in the zone **La Livinière**) tends to be higher in Syrah.

But moving inland from Narbonne, the importance of Bordeaux grapes start to grow.

In **Cabardès** the blend is > 40% Bordeaux blend (Merlot, Cabernet Sauvignon, Cabernet Franc) and 40% Rhône blend (Grenache, Syrah)

In **Malepère**, Merlot must be at least 50% of the blend while Malbec and Cabernet Franc must be at least 20%, the main grapes from Languedoc only remain accessory to the blend.

In the middle of this ocean of red wines, the Limoux stands out with its sparkling wines. **Blanquette de Limoux** is made with Mauzac and is the oldest sparkling wine in the world (it was said that Dom Perignon visited Limoux and learned sparkling winemaking technique there). **Crémant de Limoux** is Chardonnay-based (with some

Chenin Blanc and Mauzac) that must be aged 15 months on the lees. It's usually a great value for a bubbly. **Blanquette de Limoux méthode ancestrale**, the original sparkling wine, is made with 100% Mauzac.

Roussillon

Roussillon is nestled between the Pyrénées mountains and the hills of Corbières, which traps the heat and limits the amount of rain. Roussillon wines are always very concentrated, and while it still uses the same base blend as Languedoc the proportion of Mourvèdre tends to be lower and Carignan tends to be higher.

Côtes du Roussillon (and its subzone **Les Aspres**) must be blends of 3 of Carignan, Grenache, Syrah and Mourvèdre for reds and follows the Languedoc blend for whites.

Côtes du Roussillon Villages are red wines only and must be blends of 2 of Carignan, Grenache (and Lledoner Pelut), Syrah and Mourvèdre. There are 5 villages that can add their names to the appellation: **Les Aspres, Latour de France,** and **Tautavel**, where Carignan must be fermented using carbonic maceration (to round up its edges). On top of these **Garamany** and **Lesquerde** do not allow Mourvèdre.

Collioure follows the same blend and are uncomplicated red wines. **Maury sec** AOC mandates a higher proportion of grenache and 6 months of aging.

Vin doux naturels

Languedoc-Roussillon is the most prolific producer of *vin doux naturel* (fortified wines).

. . .

Several appellations along the coast produce fortified wines with Muscat Blanc à Petit Grains which are finished sweet with 16% to 20% abv. All these appellations will have Muscat in the name, and they hail from **Lunel, Mireval, Frontignan, St-Jean de Minervois,** and **Rivesaltes.** Muscat de Rivesaltes is the only appellation that also allows Muscat d'Alexandrie on top of Muscat Blanc.

In Roussillon, **Maury** and **Banyuls** craft Grenache-based VDN that have a cult following and pair well with chocolate deserts. They are made either in a reductive fashion (named *Grenat* or *Rimage*) which keeps the freshness of the fruit (like a Ruby or Vintage Port) or oxidized (named *Tuilé* or *Rancio*) to bring out dried fruit and honeyed notes (like a Tawny or Colheita Port).

15

SUD-OUEST

I f Malbec has been widely exported, other local grapes craft these unique wines.

<u>Appellations to know:</u>

Cahors AOC, **Madiran** AOC, **Jurançon** AOC, **Gaillac** AOC, **Côtes de Gascogne** IGP

Overview

South West of France tends to be overshadowed by its neighbours Bordeaux and the Languedoc. But it is home to unique wines that have developed cult followings: **Cahors**, where Malbec originates, but also **Madiran** with it's extremely grippy Tannat and the sweet **Jurançon** made with the local Gros and Petit Manseng grapes.

In recent years, the **IGP Côtes de Gascogne**, which anchors the zone of production for Armagnac, has been one of the main white wines export from France and has opened the market for these indigenous grapes beyond the French borders.

Geography, grapes and styles

Cahors, Lot & Garonne

The red wines of **Cahors** AOC are deeply coloured (nicknamed "black wines"), and they are based on Malbec (locally named Côt) with some Merlot and Tannat. While juicy and expressing aromas of plum and tobacco, they are usually more structured than Argentinian Malbec-based wines and sometimes hint of green apple.

In **Marcillac, Entraygues-le Fel, Estaing,** and **Côtes de Millau,** the wines blend in Fer Servadou, a local grape that brings a tingly acidity and tannins.

Gaillac is the most versatile appellation, and produces red, rosé, and whites that can be dry, sweet or sparkling. Reds and rosés are made from Syrah and Fer Servadou, the main one named, while whites include Len de l'el (a local grape) Mauzac and Muscadelle. Sweet wines, labelled **Gaillac doux** are very popular with the locals as a desert wine. Sparkling wines will be labeled Gaillac if made with the traditional method or **Gaillac méthode Gaillacoise** if made with the ancestral method.

Pyrénées

Further South, **Madiran** delivers a punch of Tannat, a very tannic grape that needs a few years in bottle to soften, but is a hearty accompaniment for heavier, braised meats. The reds of **Bearn** usually blend more Cabernet Franc and Cabernet Sauvignon. While **Saint-Mont** and **Tursan** also incorporate Fer Servadou.

But the region is also well known for its white wine production, especially because of **Jurançon**. These white wine are made with Gros Manseng and Petit Manseng, and while **Jurançon Sec** are finished dry, Jurançon is medium-sweet to sweet; **Jurançon "Vendange tardive"** is hand harvested and luscious. **Pacherinc du Vic-Bilh** follows a similar recipe.

Also of note is **Irouléguy**, a Basque country red wine based on Cabernet Franc and Cabernet Sauvignon, with Tannat completing the blend although destemming is mandatory to soften the tannins. The whites from Irouléguy are based on a similar formula as Jurançon

Côtes de Gascogne

The **IGP Côtes de Gascogne**, which covers a large area of the South West is the home to many value-oriented wines, crafted both from local and more common grapes. You will find whites made with Gros Manseng, Petit Manseng, Colombard and Ugni Blanc, as well as Chardonnay and Sauvignon Blanc, finished both dry and off-dry.

The reds are made with Tannat, Merlot, Cabernet Franc and Cabernet Sauvignon.

Other widely distributed wines come from the **IGP Comté Tolosan** around the town of Toulouse, which follows a similar blend.

16

BORDEAUX

C abernet Sauvignon, Merlot are the backbone of Bordeaux. But its most expensive wine is a luscious desert wine.

Appellations to know:

Bordeaux AOC, **Pauillac** AOC, **Saint-Émilion** AOC, **Medoc** AOC, **Graves** AOC, **Sauternes** AOC, *Cru classés*

Overview

With its location on the map and history, Bordeaux has been at the centre of French wine trade, with its merchants controlling the distribution worldwide. But that commercial success has led to an increase in retail price that has put the best Bordeaux wines out of reach, while also boosting the price of modest wines with the Bordeaux label on it. So is there still value to be found in Bordeaux ? Yes, if you understand where to look.

.   .   .

Bordeaux is famous for producing wines made with the so-called Bordeaux blend: Cabernet Sauvignon and Merlot, usually rounded up with Cabernet Franc and sometimes Malbec or Petit Verdot. The white Bordeaux blend is Sauvignon Blanc and Sémillon with often a touch of Muscadelle in sweet wines. But the proportion of each variety in the blend depends on where the wine is made, and makes the difference between wines that are meant to be consumed young and wines that can be cellared for decades.

Bordeaux sits at the junction of 2 rivers, the Garonne river which flows from the south of France, and the Dordogne which flows from the centre of France.

The *Rive Gauche* (left bank) of Bordeaux refers to the area between the Garonne and the Atlantic Ocean. This is where the most famous Bordeaux wines hail from and is home of Cabernet Sauvignon for reds (Médoc, Graves) and luscious sweet wines of the Sauternais.

The *Rive Droite* (right bank) is on the North side of the Dordogne river, and is heavily planted with Merlot with its flagship appellation Saint-Émilion, but where lay many of the Côtes de Bordeaux appellations. In between the 2 rivers is the 'Entre-Deux-Mer' region, known for its basic white wine although where the bulk of the Bordeaux AOC is produced.

There are 2 notable satellite regions slightly outside of the area, Bergerac along the Dordogne river and Marmande along the Garonne river which round up the picture and make wines in similar styles.

Geography, grapes and styles

Left bank

The left bank of Bordeaux is where Cabernet Sauvignon dominates the blend; this is largely due to the fact that the soil has a high gravel content (the **Graves** appellation is named for its gravel), especially since this former swamp was drained in the 1600s. This is where most well known Bordeaux wines come from, and this notoriety is widely based on the 1855 classification that ranked producers for the Paris faire into First Growth (1er Cru Classé) to Fifth Growth (5ème Cru Classé) that only included wines from the left bank, mostly from Médoc and Sauternais. While to this day the classification subsides and wines will be labeled as such (you will see "Cru Classé" on the bottle), it really only tells you that these producers have a long history of winemaking and often command a high price.

On the north side of the left bank is the area called Médoc; its 4 main villages have their own appellations

- **Pauillac:** the benchmark (the appellation of Château Lafite, Château Latour and Mouton-Rothschild)
- **Margaux:** most delicate and perfumed
- **Saint-Julien:** most 'Californian'
- **Saint-Estèphe:** most structured

While those wines will command a high price tag, they represent the best that Bordeaux has to offer. Classified growths often need to mature in the bottle before being consumed, many start to develop after 10 years and can be kept for decades, while most Bordeaux should be consumed within 5-7 years and likely before 10.

· · ·

Some better value can be found in **Moulis-En-Médoc, Listrac-Médoc** as well as **Haut-Médoc** and **Médoc**, especially with wines that bear the classification *Cru Bourgeois*. While they are not playing on the same field as the first growths, they do provide some excellent wines.

Further south, on the left bank, **Pessac-Leognan** (home of Château Haut-Brion, the only red First Growth outside of Médoc) produces very balanced wines that combine finesse and power, much like the enclosing appellation of **Graves**. But while the reds have earned the notoriety of these appellations, this is where some of the best dry white wines of Bordeaux are produced. Many producers use oak to finish their Sauvignon Blanc-Sémillon blends which stand out as age-worthy wines, and a semi-sweet version named **Graves Supérieures** AOC is a notable version of that style of wine.

But when it comes to whites, without a doubt Bordeaux's most famous wine is **Sauternes** AOC. If the most expensive wine in the world (Château d'Yquem) had its own category in the 1855 classification (Premier Cru Supérieur), it's because there is nothing that compares. The Sauvignon Blanc, Sémillon and Muscadelle blend is hand harvested, berry by berry when the right amount of botrytis affects the grapes. These lusciously sweet wines can keep for decades, and develop honey and dried fruit flavours that instead of pairing with desert can easily replace it. And even if **Sauternes** and its neighbours **Barsac** and **Cérons** usually command a high price tag, they are often found in half bottles and still remain the best value in Bordeaux.

For less expensive alternatives, a few appellations just across from the Garonne river produce a similar style of sweet wines, although for the most part a notch below except in excellent vintages: **Cadillac,**

Loupiac and Sainte-Croix-Du-Mont. While technically in the 'Entre-Deux-Mers' zone, their style is similar.

Right bank

If Cabernet Sauvignon dominates the left bank, the right bank is where Merlot shines with help from Cabernet Franc.

Saint-Émilion AOC and its higher end **Saint-Émilion Grand Cru** AOC are more rounded and silken, and exemplify the drinkability of Bordeaux even though they age well. If the 4 satellites of St-Émilion (**St. George-St. Émilion, Lussac-St. Émilion, Montagne-St. Émilion** and **Puisseguin-St. Émilion**) are less expensive, it's because they tend to be a more delicate presentation of the same flavour profile.

Pomerol bring denser aromas and more structure, and have a long potential for aging. **Lalande-de-Pomerol** tends to bring out brighter red berry flavours, as does **Fronsac** and **Canon-Fronsac**.

Côtes de Bordeaux, Côtes de Bourg, Côtes de Castillon and **Côtes de Francs** are the lower-middle tier of Bordeaux. While Merlot and Cabernet Franc dominate the blend, some Cabernet Sauvignon is used. On the same level, **Blaye, Côtes de Blaye** and **Premières Côtes de Blayes** reds follow the same recipe, but the whites often include Ugni Blanc (Trebbiano) and Colombard.

Entre-Deux-Mers

Premières Côtes de Bordeaux, Côtes de Bordeaux-Cadillac, and **Côtes de Bordeaux-Saint Macaire** use the same Merlot-dominated blend for reds, but the whites are made with Sauvignon Blanc, Sémillon and Muscadelle and can range from dry to sweet.

. . .

Entre-Deux-Mers is reserved for dry whites, made with mostly Sauvignon Blanc in a way that tends to mute its aromatics, with some Sémillon.

But this is the part of Bordeaux that produces the bulk of the **Bordeaux** AOC and **Bordeaux Supérieur** AOC, which covers the entire region of Bordeaux. This is the low end of Bordeaux, so the quality of the wine varies widely, and is often the source of disappointments.

Bordeaux Supérieur has more restrictions on yield and minimum alcohol, so the wines tend to be of a slightly higher quality. For red, it also means a mandatory aging of 9 months, but for whites it means that they are finished semi-sweet or sweet.

Bergerac and Marmandais

While Bordeaux AOC can be overpriced, much better value can be found up the Dorgogne river in **Bergerac** AOC. The region crafts wine similar in style to Bordeaux with the same set of grapes, and can easily be confused for a Bordeaux. The reds and rosés are sold under the **Bergerac** AOC, while **Bergerac Sec** AOC is for dry whites and **Côtes de Bergerac** AOC for sweet wines and superior red wines.

For a more robustly structured wine, **Pécharmant** AOC brings Malbec to the mix and provides a deeply coloured wine with high potential for aging.

But **Montbazillac** AOC may be Bergerac's best kept secret. Its hand harvested luscious whites follow the same blend as Sauternes, although often with a higher proportion of Muscadelle and the resulting wine is delightfully fresh when young and complex when aged. **Saussignac** and **Rosette**, as well as **Côtes de Montravel** and **Haut-Montravel** are made in the same style, although not always as successful.

Montravel is reserved for dry whites and a few reds, in the same style as Entre-Deux-Mers.

In a similar fashion, going up the Garonne rivers are the appellations of the Marmandais which follow the Bordeaux formula. **Buzet** is the closest, although, **Côtes du Marmandais** and **Côtes de Duras** reds could easily pass for a Bordeaux, while their whites include more Ugni Blanc and other grapes.

PART III

LOOKING FOR A WINE

17

MAPS OF VARIETIES

The following pages will help you locate which regions grow which grapes.

While some varieties can be found in large areas, remember that the same grape at a higher latitude in a cooler climate will be more acidic and light bodied.

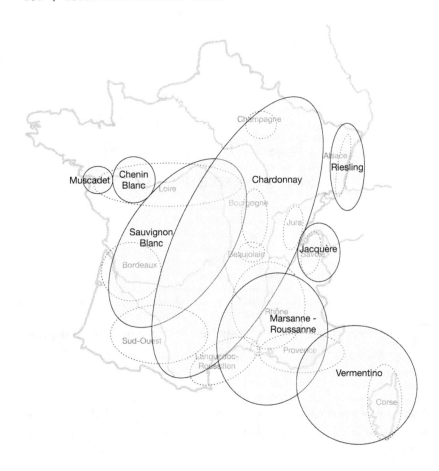

Overview of the main French white grape varieties

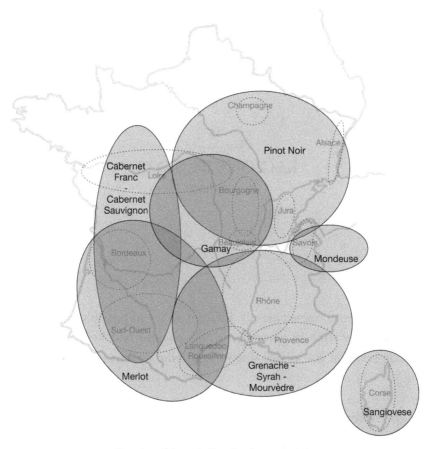

Overview of the main French red grape varieties

18

REGIONS BY STYLE

IF YOU LIKE...

O f course, wines are all different so it's impossible to find the same wine in two places. This chapter will help you find a starting point if you are looking for a specific style wine.

Light, refreshing, non-aromatic white

If you like Italian Pinot Grigio, especially from the Alps, try a **Muscadet** from the Loire valley, or a **Picpoul de Pinet** from Languedoc.

Full body, fresh non-aromatic white

If you like Chenin Blanc from South Africa, try **Savennières** or **Vouvray**, both Loire valley Chenin Blanc.

Chablis, with its mineral acidity brings also the body of unoaked Chardonnay, especially in the *premier cru* and *grand cru*. Or you can go for a **Graves** from Bordeaux where the Sauvignon is understated and Sémillon dominates the blend.

. . .

Full body, powerful oaky white

If you like California Chardonnay, or love oak with your white, go for **Bourgogne** wines, from a **Meursault** to any of the *grand cru* like **Charlemagne** or **Montrachet**.

Light, refreshing aromatic whites

If you like New Zealand Sauvignon blanc, try a Loire Valley white, like a **Sancerre, Quincy** or **Touraine**. For more flinty aromas, **Pouilly-Fumé** is the answer.

Full body aromatic dry whites

If you like Trocken or Grosse Gewachs Riesling from Germany, try an **Alsace Riesling**.

Off-dry whites

Vouvray from the Loire valley, and late harvest wines from **Alsace Vendanges Tardives**, especially Gewurztraminer is a first place to look.

Sweet whites

If you enjoy the floral and lychee aromas, look for a Muscat vin doux naturel (**Muscat de Rivesaltes, Muscat de Frontignan**, etc... in Languedoc).

If you like more honeyed notes, **Sauternes** and **Montbazillac** in Bordeaux, but also **Côteaux du Layon** in the Loire valley offer botrytized sweet wines.

Of course, vin de paille from **Jura** would also fit the bill.

. . .

Light, drinkable reds

Go for a **Beaujolais Villages**, or a Beaujolais cru like **Fleurie** or **Moulin-à-Vents** for an easy to drink red that is very versatile with food.

Fresh but structured reds

If you like Pinot from Oregon or New Zealand, go for a Bourgogne, especially a village appellation like **Gevrey-Chambertin** or **Santenay**. Of course, you can step it up with *premier cru* and *grand cru* which will ramp up the structure.

Medium bodied, heavily extracted reds

If you like Argentinian Malbec, you have to try the original **Cahors**, although other blends from the south west round up Merlot with Malbec, and **Pécharmant** near Bordeaux delivers this high extraction.

Peppery, full bodied bold reds

If you like Australian Shiraz, try a southern Rhône blend from **Châteauneuf-du-Pape** or **Rasteau**. If you want a more complex if less in-your-face version of that style of wine, go for a northern Rhône cru like **Côte-Rôtie** or **Crozes-Hermitage** on a warmer vintage. If you want bold, go for **Côtes du Roussillon-Villages** which never fails to pack a punch.

Powerful, tannic, full bodied reds

If you like a California Cab', you will end up in Bordeaux. If **St Julien** is the closest cousin to California, look for Cru Bourgeois or Cru Artisan in the **Médoc.** You can also look in the Languedoc with Malepère, although it may not offer the same amount of body.

19

REGIONS BY APPELLATION

This chapter contains the alphabetical list of appellations mentioned in this book indicating in which region they are discussed, followed by the Grand Crus of Alsace, then the Grand Crus of Bourgogne

Appellations

A.

- **Aloxe-Corton AOC:** (Bourgogne - Côte de Beaune)
- **Alsace AOC:** (Alsace) including the mentions *Gentil* and *Edelzwicker* and villages (**Bergheim, Blienschwiller, Coteaux du Haut-Koenigsbourg, Côtes de Barr, Côte de Rouffach, Klevener de Heiligenstein, Ottrott, Rodern, Saint-Hippolyte, Scherwiller, Vallée Noble, Val Saint Grégoire** and **Wolxheim**)
- **Alsace Grand Cru AOC:** (Alsace)
- **Anjou Coteaux de la Loire AOC** (Middle Loire)
- **Arbois AOC:** (Jura)

B.

- **Bandol AOC:** (Provence)
- **Banyuls AOC:** (Languedoc - VDN)
- **Barsac AOC:** (Bordeaux - left bank)
- **Baux de Provence AOC:** (Provence)
- **Bearn AOC:** (Sud-Ouest - Pyrénées)
- **Beaujolais AOC:** (Beaujolais)
- **Beaujolais-Villages AOC:** (Beaujolais)
- **Beaune AOC:** (Bourgogne-Côte de Beaune)
- **Bergerac AOC:** (Bordeaux - Bergerac)
- **Blanquette de Limoux AOC:** (Languedoc - Atlantic corridor)
- **Blaye AOC:** (Bordeaux - right bank)
- **Bonnezeau AOC:** (Middle Loire)
- **Bordeaux AOC:** (Bordeaux - Entre-deux-mers & regional)
- **Bordeaux Supérieur AOC:** (Bordeaux - Entre-deux-mers & regional)
- **Bourgogne AOC:** (Bourgogne - regional)
- **Bourgogne-Côte d'Or AOC:** (Bourgogne - regional)
- **Bourgogne Aligoté AOC:** (Bourgogne - regional)
- **Bourgogne Gamay AOC:** (Bourgogne - regional)
- **Bourgogne Grand Ordinaire AOC:** (Bourgogne - regional) legacy name for Coteaux Bourguignons AOC
- **Bourgogne Passe-Tout-Grains AOC:** (Bourgogne - regional)
- **Bourgueil AOC:** (Middle Loire)
- **Bouzeron AOC:** (Bourgogne - Côte Chalonnaise)
- **Brouilly AOC:** (Beaujolais - Crus)
- **Bugey AOC:** (Bugey)
- **Buzet AOC:** (Bordeaux - Marmandais)

C.

- **Cabardès AOC:** (Languedoc - Atlantic corridor)
- **Cabernet d'Anjou AOC:** (Middle Loire)

- **Cabernet de Saumur AOC:** (Middle Loire)
- **Cadillac AOC:** (Bordeaux - left bank*)
- **Cahors AOC:** (Sud-Ouest - Cahors and Lot)
- **Canon-Fronsac AOC:** (Bordeaux - right bank)
- **Cairanne AOC:** (Southern Rhône)
- **Cassis AOC:** (Provence)
- **Cérons AOC:** (Bordeaux - left bank)
- **Chablis AOC:** (Bourgogne - Chablis)
- **Chablis Grand Cru AOC:** (Bourgogne - Chablis) with 7 *climats* named **Blanchot, Bougros, Les Clos, Grenouilles, Les Preuses, Valmur** and **Vaudésir**
- **Chablis Premier Cru AOC:** (Bourgogne - Chablis)
- **Chambolle-Musigny AOC:** (Bourgogne - Côte de Nuits)
- **Champagne AOC:** (Champagne)
- **Chassagne-Montrachet AOC:** (Bourgogne - Côte de Beaune)
- **Château-Chalon AOC:** (Jura)
- **Château-Grillet AOC:** (Northern Rhône)
- **Chateauneuf-du-Pape AOC:** (Southern Rhône)
- **Chaume AOC:** (Middle Loire)
- **Chenas AOC:** (Beaujolais - Crus)
- **Chinon AOC:** (Middle Loire)
- **Chiroubles AOC:** (Beaujolais - Crus)
- **Clairette de Die AOC:** (Rhône - others)
- **Clairette du Languedoc AOC:** (coastal Languedoc)
- **Collioure AOC:** (Roussillon)
- **Comté Tolosan IGP:** (Sud-Ouest - Gascogne)
- **Condrieu AOC:** (Northern Rhône)
- **Corbières AOC:** (Languedoc - Atlantic corridor) with sub-zone **Boutenac**
- **Cornas AOC:** (Northern Rhône)
- **Corse AOC:** (Corse) with sub-zones **Calvi, Sartène, Figari, Porto-Vecchio, Côteaux du Cap Corse**
- **Costières de Nimes AOC:** (Rhône - others)
- **Côte de Brouilly AOC:** (Beaujolais - Crus)

- Côte-Rôtie AOC: (Northern Rhône)
- Coteaux Bourguignons AOC: (Bourgogne - regional)
- Coteaux Champenois AOC: (Champagne)
- Coteaux d'Aix-en-Provence AOC: (Provence)
- Coteaux de l'Aubance AOC: (Middle Loire)
- Coteaux de Pierrevert AOC: (Provence)
- Coteaux du Layon AOC: (Middle Loire)
- Coteaux Varois en Provence AOC: (Provence)
- Côtes de Beaune-Villages AOC: (Bourgogne-Côte de Beaune)
- Côtes de Bergerac AOC: (Bordeaux - Bergerac)
- Côtes de Blaye AOC: (Bordeaux - right bank)
- Côtes de Montravel AOC: (Bordeaux - Bergerac)
- Côtes de Bordeaux AOC: (Bordeaux - right bank)
- Côtes de Bordeaux-Cadillac AOC: (Bordeaux - Entre-deux-mers)
- Côtes de Bordeaux-Saint Macaire AOC: (Bordeaux - Entre-deux-mers)
- Côtes de Bourg AOC: (Bordeaux - right bank)
- Côtes de Castillon AOC: (Bordeaux - right bank)
- Côtes de Duras AOC: (Bordeaux - Marmandais)
- Côtes de Francs AOC: (Bordeaux - right bank)
- Côtes de Gascogne IGP: (Sud-Ouest - Gascogne)
- Côtes de Millau AOC: (Sud-Ouest - Cahors and Lot)
- Côtes de Nuits-Villages AOC: (Bourgogne - Côte de Nuits)
- Côtes du Jura AOC: (Jura)
- Côtes du Marmandais AOC: (Bordeaux - Marmandais)
- Côtes du Rhône AOC: (Southern Rhône)
- Côtes du Rhône Villages AOC: (Southern Rhône)
- Côtes du Roussillon AOC: (Roussillon) with sub-zone **Les Aspres**
- Côtes du Roussillon Villages AOC: (Roussillon) with sub-zones **Les Aspres, Latour de France, Tautavel, Garamany** and **Lesquerde**

- Côtes du Vivarais AOC: (Rhône - others)
- Côtes de Provence AOC: (Provence) with 4 sub-zones (Sainte-Victoire, Fréjus, La Londe and Pierrefeu)
- Coulanges-La-Vineuse AOC: (Bourgogne - Chablis & Grand Auxerrois)
- Crémant d'Alsace AOC: (Alsace)
- Crémant de Bourgogne AOC: (Bourgogne - regional)
- Crémant de Limoux AOC: (Languedoc - Atlantic corridor)
- Crémant de Loire AOC: (Middle Loire)
- Crozes-Hermitage AOC: (Northern Rhône)

E.

- Entraygues-le Fel AOC: (Sud-Ouest - Cahors and Lot)
- Entre-Deux-Mers AOC: (Bordeaux - Entre-deux-mers)
- Ermitage AOC: (Northern Rhône) alternative spelling for Hermitage AOC
- Estaing AOC: (Sud-Ouest - Cahors and Lot)
- L'Étoile AOC: (Jura)

F.

- Faugères AOC: (coastal Languedoc)
- Fitou AOC: (coastal Languedoc)
- Fixin AOC: (Bourgogne - Côte de Nuits)
- Fleurie AOC: (Beaujolais - Crus)
- Fronsac AOC: (Bordeaux - right bank)

G.

- Gaillac AOC: (Sud-Ouest - Cahors and Lot)
- Gevrey-Chambertin AOC: (Bourgogne - Côte de Nuits)
- Gigondas AOC: (Southern Rhône)
- Givry AOC: (Bourgogne - Côte Chalonnaise)
- Graves AOC: (Bordeaux - left bank)

- Graves Supérieures AOC: (Bordeaux - left bank)
- Grignan-lès-Adhémar AOC: (Rhône - others)
- Gros Plant du Pays Nantais AOC: (Lower Loire)

H.

- Haut-Médoc AOC: (Bordeaux - left bank)
- Haut-Montravel AOC: (Bordeaux - Bergerac)
- Hautes Côtes de Beaune AOC: (Bourgogne-Côte de Beaune)
- Hautes Côtes de Nuits AOC: (Bourgogne - Côte de Nuits)
- Hermitage AOC: (Northern Rhône)

I.

- Ile de Beauté IGP: (Corse)
- Irancy AOC: (Bourgogne - Chablis & Grand Auxerrois)
- Irouléguy AOC: (Sud-Ouest - Pyrénées)

J.

- Juliénas AOC: (Beaujolais - Crus)
- Jurançon AOC: (Sud-Ouest - Pyrénées)
- Jurançon Sec AOC: (Sud-Ouest - Pyrénées)

L.

- La Clape AOC: (coastal Languedoc)
- Ladoix-Serrigny AOC: (Bourgogne - Côte de Beaune)
- Lalande-de-Pomerol AOC: (Bordeaux - right bank)
- Languedoc AOC: (Languedoc - regional) with sub-zones Cabrières, Grés de Montpellier, La Méjanelle, Montpeyroux, Pézenas, Quatourze, Saint-Christol, Saint-Drézéry, Saint-Georges-d'Orques, Saint-Saturnin and Sommières.
- Les Baux de Provence AOC: (Provence)

- **Lirac AOC:** (Southern Rhône)
- **Listrac-Médoc AOC:** (Bordeaux - left bank)
- **Loupiac AOC:** (Bordeaux - left bank*)
- **Lubéron AOC:** (Rhône - others)
- **Lugny AOC:** (Bourgogne - Mâconnais)
- **Lussac-St. Émilion AOC:** (Bordeaux - right bank)

M.

- **Mâcon AOC:** (Bourgogne - Mâconnais)
- **Mâcon-Villages AOC:** (Bourgogne - Mâconnais)
- **Madiran AOC:** (Sud-Ouest - Pyrénées)
- **Malepère AOC:** (Languedoc - Atlantic corridor)
- **Maranges AOC:** (Bourgogne-Côte de Beaune)
- **Marcillac AOC:** (Sud-Ouest - Cahors and Lot)
- **Margaux AOC:** (Bordeaux - left bank)
- **Marsannay AOC:** (Bourgogne - Côte de Nuits)
- **Maury AOC:** (Languedoc - VDN)
- **Maury sec AOC:** (Roussillon)
- **Médoc AOC:** (Bordeaux - left bank)
- **Menetou-Salon AOC:** (Upper Loire)
- **Mercurey AOC:** (Bourgogne - Côte Chalonnaise)
- **Meursault AOC:** (Bourgogne-Côte de Beaune)
- **Minervois AOC:** (Languedoc - Atlantic corridor) with sub-zone **La Livinière**
- **Montagne-St. Émilion AOC:** (Bordeaux - right bank)
- **Montagny AOC:** (Bourgogne - Côte Chalonnaise)
- **Montbazillac AOC:** (Bordeaux - Bergerac)
- **Montlouis AOC:**(Middle Loire)
- **Montravel AOC:** (Bordeaux - Bergerac)
- **Morey Saint-Denis AOC:** (Bourgogne - Côte de Nuits)
- **Morgon AOC:** (Beaujolais - Crus)
- **Moulin-à-Vents AOC:** (Beaujolais - Crus)
- **Moulis-En-Médoc AOC:** (Bordeaux - left bank)
- **Muscadet AOC** (Lower Loire)

- Muscadet-Coteaux de la Loire AOC (Lower Loire)
- Muscadet-Côtes de Grandlieu AOC (Lower Loire)
- Muscadet-Sèvre et Maine AOC (Lower Loire) Sub-zones: Château-Thébaud, Clisson, Gorges, Goulaine, Monnières – Saint-Fiacre, Mouzillon – Tillières and Le Pallet.
- Muscat de Beaumes de Venise AOC: (Southern Rhône)
- Muscat de Frontignan AOC: (Languedoc - VDN)
- Muscat de Lunel AOC: (Languedoc - VDN)
- Muscat de Mireval AOC: (Languedoc - VDN)
- Muscat de St-Jean de Minervois AOC: (Languedoc - VDN)
- Muscat de Rivesaltes AOC: (Languedoc - VDN)
- Muscat du Cap Corse AOC: (Corse)

N.

- Nuits-Saint-George AOC: (Bourgogne - Côte de Nuits)

P.

- Pacherinc du Vic-Bilh AOC: (Sud-Ouest - Pyrénées)
- Palette AOC: (Provence)
- Patrimonio AOC: (Corse)
- Pauillac AOC: (Bordeaux - left bank)
- Pays d'Oc IGP: (Languedoc - regional)
- Pécharmant AOC: (Bordeaux - Bergerac)
- Pernand-Vergelesse AOC: (Bourgogne - Côte de Beaune)
- Pessac-Leognan AOC: (Bordeaux - left bank)
- Petit Chablis AOC: (Bourgogne - Chablis)
- Pic Saint-Loup AOC: (coastal Languedoc)
- Picpoul de Pinet AOC: (coastal Languedoc)
- Pomerol AOC: (Bordeaux - right bank)
- Pommard AOC: (Bourgogne-Côte de Beaune)
- Premières Côtes de Blayes AOC: (Bordeaux - right bank)
- Premières Côtes de Bordeaux AOC: (Bordeaux - Entre-deux-mers)

- **Pouilly-Fumé AOC:** (Upper Loire)
- **Pouilly-Fuissé AOC:** (Bourgogne - Mâconnais)
- **Pouilly-Loché AOC:** (Bourgogne - Mâconnais)
- **Pouilly-Vinzelles AOC:** (Bourgogne - Mâconnais)
- **Puisseguin-St. Émilion AOC:** (Bordeaux - right bank)
- **Puligny-Montrachet AOC:** (Bourgogne - Côte de Beaune)

Q.

- **Quarts de Chaume AOC:** (Middle Loire)
- **Quincy AOC:** (Upper Loire)

R.

- **Rasteau AOC:** (Southern Rhône)
- **Rasteau sec AOC:** (Southern Rhône)
- **Régnié AOC:** (Beaujolais - Crus)
- **Reuilly AOC:** (Upper Loire)
- **Rosé d'Anjou AOC:** (Middle Loire)
- **Rosé de Loire AOC:** (Middle Loire)
- **Rosette AOC:** (Bordeaux - Bergerac)
- **Roussette de Savoie AOC:** (Savoie)
- **Roussette du Bugey AOC:** (Bugey)
- **Rully AOC:** (Bourgogne - Côte Chalonnaise)

S.

- **Saint-Aubin AOC:** (Bourgogne-Côte de Beaune)
- **Saint-Bris AOC:** (Bourgogne - Chablis & Grand Auxerrois)
- **Saint-Chinian AOC:** (coastal Languedoc) sub-zones of Berlou and Roquebrun.
- **Saint-Émilion AOC:** (Bordeaux - right bank)
- **Saint-Émilion Grand Cru AOC:** (Bordeaux - right bank)
- **Saint-Estèphe AOC:** (Bordeaux - left bank)
- **Saint George-St. Émilion AOC:** (Bordeaux - right bank)

- Saint-Joseph AOC: (Northern Rhône)
- Saint-Julien AOC: (Bordeaux - left bank)
- Saint-Mont AOC: (Sud-Ouest - Pyrénées)
- Saint-Peray AOC: (Northern Rhône)
- Saint-Romain AOC: (Bourgogne-Côte de Beaune)
- Saint-Véran AOC: (Bourgogne - Mâconnais)
- Sainte-Croix-Du-Mont AOC: (Bordeaux - left bank*)
- Sancerre AOC: (Upper Loire)
- Saussignac AOC: (Bordeaux - Bergerac)
- Santenay AOC: (Bourgogne-Côte de Beaune)
- Sauternes AOC: (Bordeaux - left bank)
- Savennières AOC: (Middle Loire)
- Savennières-Coulée de Serrant AOC: (Middle Loire)
- Savennières-Roche aux Moines AOC: (Middle Loire)
- Savoie AOC: (Savoie) with villages for red: **Arbin, Chautagne, Chignin, Jongieux** and **St. Jean de la Porte** and for whites **Apremont, Chautagne, Chignin** and **Jongieux**
- Seyssel AOC: (Savoie)

T.

- Tavel AOC: (Southern Rhône)
- Terrasses du Larzac AOC: (coastal Languedoc)
- Touraine AOC: (Middle Loire)
- Tursan AOC: (Sud-Ouest - Pyrénées)

V.

- Vacqueyras AOC: (Southern Rhône)
- Val de Loire IGP: (Middle Loire)
- Ventoux AOC: (Rhône - others)
- Vin de Corse AOC: (Corse) see **Corse AOC**
- Vin du Pays d'Oc: (Languedoc - regional) see **Pays d'Oc IGP**
- Vinsobres AOC: (Southern Rhône)
- Viré-Clessé AOC: (Bourgogne - Mâconnais)

- **Volnay AOC:** (Bourgogne-Côte de Beaune)
- **Vosne-Romanée AOC:** (Bourgogne - Côte de Nuits)
- **Vougeot AOC:** (Bourgogne - Côte de Nuits)
- **Vouvray AOC:** (Middle Loire)

Grand Crus d'Alsace

There are 51 Grand Crus in Alsace

- Altenberg de Bergbieten
- Altenberg de Bergheim
- Altenberg de Wolxheim
- Brand
- Bruderthal
- Eichberg
- Engelberg
- Florimont
- Frankstein
- Froehn
- Furstentum
- Geisberg
- Gloeckelberg
- Goldert
- Hatschbourg
- Hengst
- Kaefferkopf
- Kanzlerberg
- Kastelberg
- Kessler
- Kirchberg de Barr
- Kirchberg de Ribeauvillé
- Kitterlé
- Mambourg

- Mandelberg
- Marckrain
- Moenchberg
- Muenchberg
- Ollwiller
- Osterberg
- Pfersigberg
- Pfingstberg
- Praelatenberg
- Rangen
- Rosacker
- Saering
- Schlossberg
- Schoenenbourg
- Sommerberg
- Sonnenglanz
- Spiegel
- Sporen
- Steinert
- Steingrubler
- Steinklotz
- Vorbourg
- Wiebelsberg
- Wineck-Schlossberg
- Winzenberg
- Zinnkoepflé
- Zotzenberg

Grand Crus de Bourgogne

There are 35 Grand crus in Bourgogne

Chablis is for white wine only, as are all Grand Crus from Côte de Beaune (except for Corton) while all Grand Crus from Côte de Nuits (except for Musigny) are for red wines only.

- Chambertin (Côte de Nuits)
- Chambertin-Clos de Bèze (Côte de Nuits)
- Chapelle-Chambertin (Côte de Nuits)
- Charmes-Chambertin (Côte de Nuits)
- Griotte-Chambertin (Côte de Nuits)
- Latricières-Chambertin (Côte de Nuits)
- Mazis-Chambertin (Côte de Nuits)
- Mazoyères-Chambertin (Côte de Nuits)
- Ruchottes-Chambertin (Côte de Nuits)
- Bonnes-Mares (Côte de Nuits)
- Clos de la Roche (Côte de Nuits)
- Clos des Lambrays (Côte de Nuits)
- Clos de Tart (Côte de Nuits)
- Clos Saint-Denis (Côte de Nuits)
- Bonnes-Mares (Côte de Nuits)
- Musigny (Côte de Nuits)
- Clos de Vougeot (Côte de Nuits)
- Échezeaux (Côte de Nuits)
- Grands Échezeaux (Côte de Nuits)
- La Grande Rue (Côte de Nuits)
- La Romanée (Côte de Nuits)
- La Tâche (Côte de Nuits)
- Richebourg (Côte de Nuits)
- Romanée-Conti (Côte de Nuits)
- Romanée-Saint-Vivant (Côte de Nuits)
- Corton (Côte de Beaune)
- Charlemagne (Côte de Beaune)
- Corton (Côte de Beaune)
- Corton-Charlemagne (Côte de Beaune)
- Corton (Côte de Beaune)
- Charlemagne (Côte de Beaune)

- Bâtard-Montrachet (Côte de Beaune)
- Bienvenues-Bâtard-Montrachet (Côte de Beaune)
- Chevalier-Montrachet (Côte de Beaune)
- Montrachet (Côte de Beaune)
- Criots-Bâtard-Montrachet (Côte de Beaune)

20

VINTAGE CHART

M ost regions undergo variations in weather patterns which affects the wine produced. As a rule of thumb, in tough vintages the good producers fare better than the rest, and good vintages tend to lessen the difference between all producers.

Like all vintage charts, this should be taken with a grain of salt as micro-climates affect each vineyard differently, but can be a starting point.

I also made the choice of only going back to the 2010 vintage as the aging conditions matter a lot for 10+ year old bottles. If you are starting to look old bottles, the variation between individual producers matters more than the vintage chart itself, and you can find specialists for each region.

Personally, I tend to ignore vintage charts unless I am comparing two bottles of the same region, and trying to figure out whether I should go for one producer or the other.

Loire

2018: Great

2017: Good

2016: Good

2015: Great

2014: Good

2013: Passable

2012: Average

2011: Average

2010: Good

Champagne

2018: Great

2017: Poor

2016: Average

2015: Great

2014: Average

2013: Good

2012: Good

2011: Average

2010: Average

Alsace

2018: Great

2017: Great

2016: Good

2015: Great

2014: Good

2013: Average

2012: Good

2011: Average

2010: Good

Jura & Savoie

2018: Good

2017: Average

2016: Good

2015: Good

2014: Good

2013: Average

2012: Average

2011: Good

2010: Good

Bourgogne

2018: Great

2017: Good

2016: Good

2015: Great

2014: Great for whites, Average for reds

2013: Average

2012: Good

2011: Passable

2010: Great

Beaujolais

2018: Great

2017: Great

2016: Good

2015: Great

2014: Good

2013: Average

2013: Good

2011: Great

2010: Good

Rhône

2018: Great

2017: Good

2016: Good

2015: Great

2014: Passable

2013: Average

2012: Good

2011: Good

2010: Great

Provence & Corsica

2018: Good

2017: Good

2016: Good

2015: Good

2014: Average

2013: Average

2012: Good

2011: Good

2010: Average

Languedoc-Roussillon

2018: Good

2017: Good

2016: Good

2015: Good

2014: Average

2013: Good

2012: Average

2011: Good

2010: Great

Bordeaux

2018: Great

2017: Average

2016: Good

2015: Good

2014: Average

2013: Poor

2012: Average

2011: Average

2010: Great

AFTERWORD

I hope this book helped you make some sense of French wine and that you will be armed with the knowledge you need to confidently pick up your next bottle of French wine.

Now go and try something new !

ACKNOWLEDGMENTS

I would like to first thank Linda McPhee, Natale Lofaro and Steve Robinson who taught me so much about wine.

Thanks to Camilo, Cody, Dale and Harry for helping me taste all the wines we could get our hands on.

This book could not have been written without the support of my wife Charlotte.

CPSIA information can be obtained
at www.ICGtesting.com
Printed in the USA
LVHW012200180522
719128LV00011B/1151